A NEWSCAST FOR THE MASSES

Great Lakes Books

A complete listing of the books in this series can be found online at wsupress.wayne.edu

A NEWSCAST FOR THE MASSES
The History of Detroit Television News

Tim Kiska

Wayne State University Press Detroit

13 12 11 10 09   5 4 3 2 1

Library of Congress Cataloging-in-Publication Data

Kiska, Tim.
   A newscast for the masses : the history of Detroit television journalism / Tim Kiska.
       p. cm. — (Great Lakes books)
   Includes bibliographical references and index.
   ISBN 978-0-8143-3302-0 (pbk. : alk. paper)
   1. Television broadcasting of news—Michigan—Detroit—History. I. Title.
   PN4899.D554K57 2009
   070.1'950977434—dc22
                                                        2008032273

Grateful acknowledgment is made to the Leonard and Harriette
Simons Endowed Family Fund for the generous support of the
publication of this volume.

Designed by Lisa Tremaine
Typeset by Keata Brewer, E.T. Lowe Publishing Company
Composed in Janson Text and Bell Gothic

To my wife, Patricia

Contents

Acknowledgments

Many people helped on this project—either directly or indirectly by example. There are too many to list, and many of them were listed in my previous book, *From Soupy to Nuts*.

At Wayne State University Press, Kathryn Wildfong, Robin DuBlanc, and Carrie Downes Teefey were spectacular.

At the University of Michigan–Dearborn, Elaine Clark, Sid Bolkosky, Bernard Klein (no longer at the university), Carolyn Kraus, Wayne Woodward, Rashmi Luthra, Troy Murphy, Susan Sheth, Deborah Smith Pollard, Ivan Kernisky, Elizabeth Fomin, Becky Wyatt, Nancy Korenchuk, Paul Hughes, Tija Spitsberg, Gabrielle Eschrich, Dan Little, Ed Bagale, and Terry Gallagher have all been wonderful to me.

At WWJ-AM, news director Rob Davidek sets a high standard in the newsroom. He's one of the best newsmen I've worked with in my career, which is approaching forty years.

I've enjoyed the company of everybody at the station. I'd like to thank Pete Kowalski, Georgeann Herbert, Bob Mundie, Sandra McNeill, Damara Anderson, Mike Campbell, Marie Osborne, Gary Lundy, Rob Sanford, Greg Bowman, Jayne Bower, Joe Donovan, Roberta Jasina, Paul Snider, Scott Ryan, Vickie Thomas, Ron Dewey, Karen Dinkins, Sonny Eliot, Beth Fisher, Murray Feldman, Marisa Fusinski, Jeff Gilbert, Chrystal Knight, Terri Lee-Sylvester, John McElroy, Bill Rapada, Tony Ortiz, Bill Stevens, Tracey Suveges, Pat Sweeting, Ray Templin, Jim Jarecki, Renee Bianchi, Pat Vitale, Florence Walton, Andy Dulecki, Marc Smith, Tom Mazawey, and Stephanie Davis.

Introduction

Detroit News reporter Armand Gebert didn't make much of the incident at the time. But, looking back, he wondered if he had just witnessed something big. Gebert, University of Michigan, class of 1950, was a *Detroit News* reporter in 1960, a veteran of Detroit's biggest newspaper. He was standing in front of the *News* offices on West Lafayette on the western edge of downtown Detroit—just across from WWJ-TV's studios—with his colleague George Walker. Recalls Gebert: "We were approached by two young boys—I'd say ten or eleven years old. They were very polite, but still young. There had been a tour going on at WWJ, and I think they had somehow escaped from their class. They asked: 'Are you reporters?' We allowed that yes, we were. We were impressed that they were impressed. Then they asked: 'What time do you come on?' I said, 'Oh, no. We're journalists, we're with the newspapers.' They replied: 'Oh, we thought you were important.'"[1]

In the minds of those two young boys, television had eclipsed newspapers as a mass medium. It would take time for that message to sink in to the journalism community in general. In 1970 the *Detroit Free Press* newsroom had only one television set to monitor broadcast news—a silent indication that the newspaper's editors held the medium in contempt, or did not take it seriously. That television receiver was a rickety old portable set with a broken antenna that rested on a gunmetal gray typewriter stand. The set was located at a window pointing north—necessary for better reception.[2] By the year 2007, each of Detroit's two major newspapers had several panels of expensive color television sets. The *News* had six perched above the city desk, another four above the national desk, another panel in the sports department, and another in the features department. The *Free Press* had a collection of forty-one color television sets scattered around its newsroom at 615 West Lafayette—in the same building where Gebert had worked forty-seven years earlier.[3] The gunmetal typewriter stand is long gone. Instead, all of the color sets are wired for cable television. The connection extends to journalistic content. In 2006 the *Free Press* and WDIV-TV announced a partnership. *Detroit Free Press* reporters often appear on

WDIV-TV newscasts. The two organizations share polling data and journalistic information.[4]

There is no longer any doubt that local television is an important news medium. It is the biggest source of regular information for many people and an important revenue stream for the country's mighty broadcast conglomerates. Local television news has become a journalistic center of gravity, with networks aping techniques developed by local television stations. And it has become something of a cultural force.

It has come a long way from the days when the term "local television journalism" was an oxymoron. So how did the medium grow from a curiosity into a journalistic force within thirty years?

The medium grew because it followed public tastes, giving people exactly the kind of news they wanted. McHugh and Hoffman, Inc., a Detroit-based research firm that created the local television news consulting industry, told its clients that people wanted news "presented in a palatable way, easy to comprehend and with the harshness of everyday events 'softened' for them."[5] The firm's researchers told its television clients that no serious demand existed for public service programming. The firm further argued that most newsrooms were populated by college-educated journalists, whose natural inclination would be to produce a newscast for other college-educated viewers. Since less than 40 percent of the U.S. adult population over the age of twenty-five has a college education, McHugh and Hoffman urged television station managers to program newscasts for a wider range of viewers—the "Joe Six-Packs" of the world. The fact of the matter is that programming for Joe Six-Pack worked. It worked so well at WJBK-TV that the better-financed WXYZ-TV literally bought the station's frontline staff and continued on that path—a strategy that remains in place to this day.

This is a microhistory of television news, telling the bigger story of this branch of electronic journalism by relating the smaller tale of Detroit television. This book will focus on the direction of television news in metropolitan Detroit between 1947 and 1982. It will examine the ownership of Detroit's television stations, how business strategies influenced allocation of resources to television newsrooms, and how journalism developed into a profit center. The study stops in 1982 because that is when cable television, which has done so much to change television in the last two decades, began to appear in the area.[6] An epilogue will briefly survey developments between 1982 and 2007.

By the year 2007, sixty years after television's birth as a mass medium, television news has become a personality-driven product. It is a revenue generator. It is often the only local programming aired by many television stations. In Detroit, the last locally produced, daily nonnews program went off the air in 1995.

Although critics are harsh on local news, surveys show that local television news is the preferred source of information for a majority of Americans. Consider the most recent study of news consumer habits by the Pew Research Center for the People and the Press (see appendix, table 1). The Pew Center's survey demonstrated that local TV news outranks the nightly network news as a routine resource for information on current affairs. This has been true for many years, as surveys show. Although the popularity of local television news dropped 23 percent during the years 1993 to 2006, that's nowhere near the decline of network news—which lost more than half its regular viewers during the same time period. Local television still outranks its closest competitor, cable news, by a 20 percent margin.

To the millions of "regular" Americans who flock to the shopping malls and video stores, the local television news personality is a major celebrity. In Detroit, for instance, WDIV-TV anchorwoman Carmen Harlan was called upon in 2002 to host Detroit mayor Kwame Kilpatrick's swearing-in ceremony. Harlan, a twenty-year veteran of television news, looked more like a game-show host than a journalist. But it was an illustration of how television news has morphed into something beyond journalism.

Television news is where the money is. Consider these estimates from the Radio-Television News Directors Association regarding where television stations make their money. As illustrated in table 2 (see appendix), it's in news. Roughly 40 percent of television station revenue in 2001 came from news broadcasts.

Taken together, tables 1 and 2 illustrate two points: Local TV news is enormously popular, and it is also enormously important to a television station's revenue base. The point of this book is not to pass judgment on the general quality of local television news. The point is to study how it morphed into the kind of product it has become.

Among the questions to be answered are: How did television station managers go about drawing larger audiences? What were the strategies they used to develop audiences? What were the implications for journalism?

Detroit is a reasonable choice for study. It's a large midwestern city with a demographically diverse audience. At one time it was the fifth-largest television market in the country. (It is now the eleventh largest.) The ownership of Detroit's television stations also makes it worthy of study. Throughout the history of television broadcasting, legislators and industry analysts have concerned themselves with the topic. They have been uneasy about the possibility of a small group of corporations cornering the market on information and possibly subverting the democratic process. Newspaper cross-ownership of television stations, the number of television stations a TV network may own, and the number of TV station licenses the FCC may grant a company have been matters of continual debate since the advent of television. These concerns led to a ban on newspaper ownership of TV stations in 1978, although then-current owners were grandfathered in. For many years the FCC limited network ownership of television stations to five.

Detroit television had one of each kind of ownership. The Evening News Association, which owned the *Detroit News*, also owned WWJ-TV, Detroit's NBC affiliate, between 1947 and 1978. The American Broadcasting Company, owner of the ABC Television Network, owned WXYZ-TV between 1948 and 1985, when ABC sold the station to Scripps-Howard. And Storer Broadcasting Company, one of the early broadcasting conglomerates, owned WJBK-TV, Detroit's CBS affiliate, between 1948 and 1985. (The station is now owned by the Fox Stations Group, which is affiliated with Rupert Murdoch's News Corporation) As of 2008, corporate conglomerates owned all of Detroit's major television stations.

At the beginning of the twenty-first century, some journalism experts see a decline in the quality of local news. They attribute this deterioration to a lack of financial resources. The critics ascribe dwindling financial resources to the efforts of the *Fortune* 500 companies, which own the stations, to stretch profits. "What we are seeing is a clear pattern of stations being asked to stretch their products thinner and to do more with less. Over the past five years we have seen a drop in enterprise reporting—reporters going out and doing in-depth investigations in their communities and even in sending reporters to the scene of a story," reported Amy Mitchell in a presentation at Columbia University in early 2003.[7] Mitchell's group, the Project for Excellence in Journalism, noticed a 60 percent drop in investigative reporting, a nearly one-third dip in the number of stories with reporters at the scene.

But the numbers seem to indicate that viewers—in general—don't care. Local television news has maintained a following among viewers even a time when the network news audience is declining. Local television news has a particular hold among less educated viewers. It's a major source of news for 71 percent of viewers who didn't finish high school. But even among viewers with postgraduate degrees, the figure stood at 42 percent.[8]

This study traces the development of television news, both nationally and in Detroit. Pioneers such as CBS's William S. Paley went into broadcast news during the 1930s for the prestige it brought to a wild young medium. Radio journalism acquitted itself well during World War II. As television developed during the 1950s, it grew up similarly to radio: first as a backwater, then as a serious form of journalism. By the mid- to late 1960s, however, a significant change took place in the standing of television news—it was no longer a money loser. When that happened, television news' order of battle changed. Anchors were hired for reasons that had nothing to do with journalism, and were treated accordingly. They became celebrities. Most had agents who negotiated contracts for them, just as movie stars did. And news executives, with marching orders to gather the biggest possible audience, changed the character of news. This book explains how that happened.

It will begin by analyzing radio news as it developed both nationally and in Detroit during the 1920s and 1930s. Radio news did not begin as a profit center. CBS chairman William S. Paley hired two men to help CBS gain prestige in its battle against the better entrenched National Broadcasting Company. In Detroit, news was included as a promotional element for the Evening News Association. World War II demanded a better class of news broadcaster, and the radio industry rose to the occasion. The public held broadcast news in high regard as World War II ended. As chapter 1 will explain, personality has always been a major component of broadcast news. The chapter will also demonstrate how radio news began as something of a model for television.

Chapter 2 will examine television's early days, outlining the corporate positions of each of Detroit's three major television players during the era and the financial and technical pressures involved in the development of television news. Chapters 3 and 4 will deal with Detroit television journalism during the 1960s, the medium's most important growth period. The chapters will examine corporate developments and also how Detroit's television station covered the 1967 riot.

Chapter 5 will explore the development of "Happy Talk," a name given to the introduction of entertainment elements in local television news. The study will inspect the corporate and financial reasons behind the development of this phenomenon and the positive audience reaction to it. The book will show how the positive response caused the phenomenon to grow.

Chapter 6 will look at WWJ-TV's reaction to the 1967 Detroit riot, the 1960s, and developments in local television news. The station lost much of its news audience as it failed to deal with the changing realities of television. Finally, in chapter 7, the book will cover the entry of *Post-Newsweek* into the Detroit television market, the company's difficulties once it got here, and how WJBK-TV lost its news leadership.

Some would say that local TV news has turned into a circus—and a violent one, at that. *If It Bleeds, It Leads: An Anatomy of Television News* analyzes two and one-half hours of local news, advising readers that "it is a pretend medium." Matthew R. Kerbel taped newscasts during the week of February 24, 1997, from four local television stations, including Detroit's WXYZ-TV, and recorded what he saw. Kerbel, a former television newswriter, presents an extraordinarily glum account. "All that matters is that local news presents us with an endless assortment of fire, murder, assault, shootout, and accident stories, along with a host of features about things that are independent of specific events and therefore not bound by time."[9] Kerbel's book would be funny if the subject matter were not so sad. The Rocky Mountain Media Watch, a Denver-based journalism watchdog organization, studied local newscasts from across the country during the 1990s. A summary of the fourth annual survey in 1998 reported that "the news is out of balance on many stations, with an over-emphasis on crime and disaster coverage."[10]

Nationally, scholars have only begun to study local television news. Arizona State University's Craig Allen broke ground with *News Is People*, a look at news in local markets, including Philadelphia, Chicago, Cleveland, and Los Angeles.[11] Allen gained access to the files of McHugh and Hoffman,

Inc., the first and—for a time— biggest television news consulting firm in the country. McHugh and Hoffman, working with sociologists from Harvard University and the University of Chicago, developed a class-based analysis of television viewership. The firm encouraged newsroom managers to program news for the masses—not for the elite.

Locally, the literature of Detroit television journalism is slim. Dick Osgood, who worked at both WXYZ radio and WXYZ television, wrote *W*Y*X*I*E Wonderland*, an "unauthorized diary" of his years at the station.[12] On the plus side, Osgood provides a gossipy look at what went on in the station. On the negative side, Osgood cannot get a name right.[13] Osgood also recounts lengthy swatches of conversations, and although these are recounted directly from firsthand sources, it is difficult to believe that even a person blessed with an outstanding memory could recall such lengthy conversations years after the fact.

Television personalities John Kelly and Marilyn Turner chronicled their respective troubled first marriages, their troubled courtship, and occasionally troubled marriage to each other. However, they also dealt with life in the trenches of Detroit television journalism.[14] More recently, author Gordon Castelnero's *TV Land—Detroit* covered the history of entertainment and children's programming in local Detroit television.[15] However, he dealt little with television journalism.

Don F. DeGroot, who worked at or managed WWJ-TV and/or WWJ-AM for roughly four decades until 1976, wrote his memoirs, *Living on Air*.[16] The memoir was distributed mostly among family and friends, although one copy resides at the University of Maryland's Library of American Broadcasting. Most of the book concerns family matters, with only a few dozen pages devoted to his stewardship of WWJ-TV during the 1970s.

The *Detroit Free Press* and *Detroit News* covered the Detroit television industry from its birth, placing full-time reporters on the television beat from the 1950s onward. During the 1990s each newspaper had as many as three reporters, including the author, covering television. Nationally, *Broadcasting* magazine faithfully chronicled developments in the business from the perspective of station owners. The *New York Times* covered the television industry, both from a critical viewpoint and from a news perspective.

But the ephemeral nature of television news is a problem for the historian. The scripts from the early years are gone. As far as can be determined, the only Detroit television scripts that have been preserved from before 1995 are in the Lyndon Baines Johnson Presidential Library, the residue of Johnson's National Commission on Civil Disorder. The kinescopes and/or tapes of the newscasts are gone. Only a few shards of tape remain.

Until now, interviews with reporters, cameramen, and news directors who worked in Detroit television news are the only way of piecing together what happened in the industry. The author interviewed dozens of newsroom employees. Although their recollections of specific events were occasionally murky, their candor about those years was invigorating. Everybody interviewed remembered the past fondly and was happy to talk. Almost to a person, they hate what has happened to television news in Detroit.

In 2007 McHugh and Hoffman, Inc. opened its files to scholars. The company's research provides valuable insight into what Detroit television viewers were thinking about news in their city. Although the firm conducted research for WJBK-TV, McHugh and Hoffman never sugarcoated its message for the client's comfort. The company's reports will act as a Greek chorus throughout this book.

As to printed sources, the Federal Communications Commission tracked revenue in the Detroit television and radio markets until 1980, although information from several years is missing. A 1956 congressional investigation into network television practices revealed WXYZ-TV's balance sheet from the period between 1953 and 1955. Annual reports from the American Broadcasting Company and Storer Broadcasting between the 1950s and 1970s do not break out the financial performances of individual stations. The Evening News Association, a company that rarely allowed its stock to be sold outside of the two families that owned the company, never released financial figures. The author, in the course of his duties as television critic at the *Detroit News* between 1990 and 2002, collected Arbitron ratings books dating to 1974. Those manuals provide valuable estimates of who watched television news, although Arbitron provides no explanation about why people watched.

The University of Maryland's Library of American Broadcasting proved to be a treasure trove of information. The library is the official repository of the National Association of Broadcasters' collection of documents, which includes a compilation of often-obscure FCC and industry documents.

This book traces the rise of broadcast journalism in a major urban center, exploring the business reasons why companies acted the way they did running the television newsrooms in Detroit, Michigan. This work is based on the author's PhD dissertation. The biographical profiles of television personalities in that work later appeared in *From Soupy to Nuts: A History of Detroit Television,* and are revised in the current book.[17] What happens in television news is important, influencing as it does the elections of governors, U.S. senators, and members of Congress. But more important, local television explains to viewers what is happening in their communities. Network television anchors may be important because they are explaining what happens in the world. But local anchors are important because they explain what is happening on Main Street.

The epilogue to this book will explain that television stations are succeeding because they are giving viewers what they want. The purpose of this book is to explain how news went from Edward R. Murrow to car crashes and drive-by shootings.

1. EARLY RADIO

Establishing Precedents

Veteran television anchorman David Brinkley described early television news as "a journalism form that sprang naked from the sky, with no history, no customs, no style book, no past."[1] Brinkley was wrong. Television news in Detroit and elsewhere has its roots in radio journalism. Early television news programs ran fifteen minutes, an inheritance from radio news. The style of writing for a television newscast, so different from traditional newspaper writing, has its foundations in radio news. Most important, early radio news, particularly during the World War II era, provided a respectable framework for the development of television news.

Radio started out as an amusement. The men who governed radio decided that the addition of journalism would make it something more than that, garnering respect for the upstart medium. Although many of radio's pioneer newsmen were quite attractive to the public, their most important assets were their journalistic skill and their ability to think and write. Their work during World War II made the airwaves an important medium of news.

Radio came to Detroit, Michigan, on August 31, 1920. In the words of the *Detroit News*, owner of WWJ-radio:

> The sending of the election returns by the *Detroit News'* radiophone Tuesday night was fraught with romance and must go down in the history of man's conquest of the elements as a gigantic step in his progress. In the four hours that the apparatus, set up in an out-of-the-way corner of the *News* Building, was hissing and whirring its message into space, few realized that a dream and a prediction had come true. The news of the world was being given forth through this invisible trumpet to the waiting crowds in the unseen market place.[2]

Despite the talk of heady progress, radio was, in the words of CBS's William S. Paley, "a gadget, a toy, an amusing instrument of light entertainment."[3] WWJ's 1922 program schedule reflected an interest in culture, talk, and utilitarian information. The station aired time signals from the

1

U.S. Naval Observatory weekdays between 11:52 a.m. and noon, broadcast a daily weather report between 3:30 p.m. and 3:40 p.m., and gave "market quotations" between 3:40 p.m. and 4:15 p.m. The market reports included quotes from the Detroit Stock Exchange, livestock and grain reports from Chicago and elsewhere, and Wall Street's closing prices. In a 1922 book about the founding of WWJ, the *Detroit News* radio staff profiled the sixteen members of the *Detroit News* Orchestra, which played nightly, and, according to the book, was "the first radio orchestra ever organized." (Two reporters were pictured among the ten-member WWJ-radio staff in the station's promotional book.)[4]

One of the early stars of the station was *News* drama critic Al Weeks, the "Town Crier," who was known more for his wit and humor than for his dissemination of news. But Weeks was a serious professional. In 1924 he wrote *The Style Book of the Detroit News*, which coached reporters and editors on everything from language usage to journalism ethics. But it was Weeks's ability as a "dramatist and actor as well as wag" that drew the crowds and was most valuable to his employer. "At first, he held to the traditions of bellmen [town criers who gathered crowds by ringing a bell], and gave a nightly digest of the day's news, with running comment. His whimsicality was so appealing that fancy took precedence over fact."[5]

Although intended as a description of Weeks's work, the quoted comment may serve as a general sketch of the medium's first decade. Radio, at first, was not considered a serious vehicle for journalism. "The broadcasting of news on a daily basis as we know it today was not a feature of radio in the 1920s," wrote historian George H. Douglas.[6] This is ironic because the *News* was but one of many newspaper companies dabbling in radio in 1922. They included the *Atlanta Journal, Deseret News, San Francisco Examiner, Los Angeles Examiner, Minnesota Tribune*, and the *Portland Oregonian*. Even the *Detroit Free Press* jumped into the game of radio and radio news, but only haphazardly. Radio work was seen, according to historian Erik Barnouw, as a way of publicizing newspapers.[7] The new medium's managers were interested in growing an audience for radio, and the best way to do this was by offering entertainment and sports.

This was true nationally, and it was true in Detroit. The leading newscaster for WWJ-AM during the 1920s and 1930s was a man who combined journalism with a quirky sense of entertainment. He was Curtis Custer

"C. C." Bradner—known as "Brad" to his colleagues. He was native of St. Johns, Michigan, and the son of a Civil War veteran who had served in a brigade led by General George A. Custer. A veteran of the *Flint Journal* and Associated Press, Bradner had worked as a reporter at the *Detroit News* since 1910 before moving to the newspaper's broadcast operation. From the Associated Press, he had learned the power of clarity and brevity. "He never thought of himself as a practitioner of the strange new art of broadcasting," according to Weeks, Bradner's colleague at both WWJ-AM and the *News*, "It was rather that he was a writer and what he had to write was communicated to his audience not by written but by spoken word."[8] His broadcasts were laced with a sense of humor. He was described at the time of his death as a "madcap wit" and "raconteur."[9] "The routine happenings of the day, as detailed in his newscasts, were never routine, never banal," according to another account. "[A]n artful word, a droll turn of phrase interpolated here and there, set them quite apart."[10]

Harry Bannister, one of Bradner's former bosses, described Bradner's strengths and weaknesses: "His diction was not too good; he had ill-fitting false teeth which clicked audibly; he was short of breath and wheezy, totally lacking in a sense of timing; yet the man was phenomenal. Every broadcast contained a phrase, or a sentence, or an observation, worthy of repetition and remembrance."[11]

Bradner became something of a local hero. Although Bannister did not supply ratings information, he added: "Just about everybody in town listened to Brad, whose standing with the audience, as revealed by his ratings over a ten-year period, has, as far as I know, never been approached by any newscaster anywhere. His network contemporaries, men like Lowell Thomas, Edwin C. Hill, Gabriel Heatter, were all miles behind Brad in popularity."[12]

The depth and breadth of his popularity could be measured by the crowd that gathered for his funeral in 1940:

The line began to form shortly before noon and by 11:00 p.m. thousands had filed silently through the chapel. By early evening the procession was a chain of humanity of all races, ages, colors and nationalities. A little boy had walked from far out on the West Side. A brother of Mr. Bradner took him in hand and saw that he got home safely. A Negro woman passed and paused to explain that she had listened to Brad as she washed clothes day after day. An Italian woman told of learning to speak English by listening to him.[13]

Bradner was initially heard at 12:30 p.m. and 6:30 p.m. daily. But news was becoming so popular that news broadcasts were added at 7:30 a.m. and 11:00 p.m. in 1934. WWJ's 11:00 p.m. newscast was said to be the first in Detroit at that hour, a convention that would continue into the television era. Advertisers were eager to sponsor the news broadcasts. The addition of the two newscasts, however, created a problem. When Bradner was heard only twice daily, he would rewrite the *Detroit News* and/or wire dispatches. "I had seen Curt at his desk preparing his noon and dinner-hour broadcasts by cutting stories out of the daily papers, typing a few transitions, and taking his batch of notes into the studio for his newscast," recalled Fran Harris, Bradner's contemporary.[14] Bradner, a talented writer, would remold the wire services pieces to the extent that few were wise to his theft. But when sponsors were found for the two additional Detroit newscasts, Bannister was certain that they would demand something more than a rewrite job. This was a problem facing radio stations across the country. Where to get the material? Not from Associated Press, which had banned the use of its material at radio stations after a messy fight that said much about newspaper owners and the new medium.

Newspaper owners were of mixed minds about the new medium. As previously mentioned, some had eagerly invested in radio. They thought of radio as a marvelous promotional tool, and used it as such. Notice, for instance, that the orchestra in place at WWJ in 1922 was not the "WWJ Orchestra." It was the *Detroit News* Orchestra." Circulation numbers told the story of radio's power elsewhere. The *New York World* funded a nationwide radio broadcast of election returns during the evening of the 1928 presidential election, in cooperation with other newspapers. The *World* reported the biggest weekday morning circulation in its history. The *Newark Evening News*, which aired election returns via WOR during the same evening, saw its circulation almost double. "Radio helped to stimulate interest," said Arthur Sinnott, the newspaper's managing editor, "but it was only one of many factors which caused the increased circulation. We don't believe in publishing extras and engaged the radio to take the place of this form of enterprise on election night."[15]

4

But it occurred to some newspaper owners that radio might compete for advertising dollars that previously had gone directly to publishers. That realization dawned after two incidents in 1928. Dodge Motor Company publicized its new Victory Six automobile, hiring public relations wizard Edward Bernays and spending $70,000 on a gaudy, star-studded radio program. The show reached an audience of 20 million people. Advertisers noticed the success. "Only the national advertiser, under our system of private enterprise, really had the power to finance broadcasting," wrote Russell J. Hammargren, "and when radio began to compete on a national scale for the attention and for the dollars that had previously belonged exclusively to the printed message, then the period of press-radio conflict can be said to have begun."[16] The 1928 presidential campaign drove home the point, as if it needed to be emphasized. The Republican Party spent $400,000 on radio broadcasts of Herbert Hoover's political speeches, the Democrats about $600,000 on behalf of Governor Al Smith.[17]

At this point, the publishers, who saw their dollars melting away, tried to strangle the new medium in its cradle. The Associated Press, the news cooperative that was controlled by newspaper publishers, forbade radio stations from using its material, touching off the "Press War" of 1932–35. As the Pennsylvania Publishers Association wrote in a resolution, "Some broadcasting stations are already calling themselves newspapers of the air, filching local and press association news from newspapers without either consent or credit and selling time to advertisers on the strength of broadcasting the news that they purloined."[18] Ralph Casey, editor of *Journalism Quarterly*, later commented on the matter: "They [the newspaper publishers] had seen their linage decreased during the later Depression period, and attributed the rise of linage in the radio as part of this picture. . . . I think the Depression was partly responsible for decreased newspaper linage."[19] United Press planned to supply CBS with election returns in 1932, but relented under pressure from newspaper publishers. The Associated Press officially decided the next year not to sell news to radio stations, causing CBS to build its own operation with stringers. The wire services eventually did supply radio stations with news, but only after competing services, including Transradio Press, began filling the vacuum.[20]

Casey later told a congressional committee that newspapers had "saved radio from falling solely into mere showmanship" and described newspaper owners' interest in buying radio stations as one that was mutually convenient.[21] The newspaper received another outlet for promotion for its journalistic work; the radio station received a powerful benefactor. The two media, in that way, converged. As Frank Luther Mott, a Pulitzer Prize–winning journalism educator, told a congressional committee investigating links between the newspaper and radio industries in 1941: "It seems to me that the newspaper offers radio economic stability, trained personnel (and that covers a good deal I won't go into) and a tradition of respect for the news and ability in handling it. Radio offers the newspaper outlet for material which it has gathered, and economic stability, the advertising field, and so on. And, also, the radio offers the newspaper a challenging opportunity in the new technological medium."[22]

It turned out that William E. Scripps, publisher of the *Detroit News* and son of the newspaper's founder, James Scripps, was in the forefront of the new technology. Newspapers owners, for the most part, exhibited a curiosity about radio and treated it as a strange new breed of animal that deserved attention. But when the owners realized the animal cost them money, they turned negative. After realizing an affinity of interests, newspaper owners quickly changed their minds. "The largest number of stations licensed to a single class of business or persons affiliated with such a business seems to be that of newspaper owned or affiliated stations," the FCC reported.[23] Newspapers owned twenty-eight of the country's radio stations by the late 1930s.

Radio commentators appeared to pose the biggest threat to the newspaper industry's hegemony. Early radio audiences seemed fascinated by them, the noisier the better. A single commentator was less expensive than an entire news department, but could be plenty damaging to a newspaper. As related in a 1970 study of the press-radio conflict, Roy Howard of the Scripps Howard newspaper chain thought commentators were the most dangerous men in radio. He told his colleagues "that the main issue toward which the publishers should address themselves was the commentators, as opposed to the news announcers, who skimmed the news from papers and then broadcast it before the papers could reach the public."[24] Detroit commentator Jerry Buckley illustrated the attraction of flashy commentary. Gerald Buckley had no previous journalistic experience before becoming a broadcaster, but he had experience with investigative techniques, having worked for Henry Ford as an investigator. Buckley, every bit as angered as Ford at the decline of morals in his day, hammered away at corruption and bootlegging in Detroit, using his program on Detroit's WMBC to campaign for the ouster of Detroit mayor Charles Bowles. Buckley thumped for a cleanup of the city. "We are sick and tired of the ring and the graft, of the four-flushers, of the exploitation of the city by opportunists," Buckley proclaimed in a typical 1930 broadcast.[25] Voters ultimately recalled Bowles. However, Buckley was gunned down in the lobby of Detroit's La Salle Hotel within hours of announcing the results.[26] His funeral was among the most well attended ever seen in Detroit, and made him more famous and powerful in death than he had been in life.

But another line of thought was developing, one that would have an enduring and powerful influence on the medium of radio specifically and journalism in general. CBS's William S. Paley decided in the late 1920s and early 1930s that news was the new medium's ticket to respectability. Journalism would be separate from cultural and entertainment broadcasting: "At CBS, my associates and I recognized radio news as a unique service we could provide to the public, and we realized early that the prestige of our network would depend to a considerable extent upon how well we could provide such service. It seemed to me that if radio could broadcast the news of the day and special events, it would be a highly desirable service to the more serious listeners."[27]

Paley's newsroom hiring policies reflected the distinction between journalism and entertainment. At least in the newsroom, a good voice and slick presentation would be subordinate to brains and newsgathering skills. "In hiring men for the CBS newsroom, we would favor the good newsman over the pleasant speaking voice," Paley wrote. "I became convinced that journalistic judgment was far more important in a radio newsman than any other quality. All of our future hiring at CBS News would reflect that very early decision."[28] Paley hired two men to make the decision stick: Paul White and Edward Klauber. Paley hired Klauber, a former *New York Times* night city editor, in 1930. Klauber had already become something of a legend at the *Times* before joining CBS. "Both as a reporter and rewrite man, Mr. Klauber was known to his colleagues as a perfectionist with his copy who regarded newspaper work as deserving of the highest ethical standards," his old newspaper, the *Times*, wrote after he died.[29] Although Paley brought in Klauber to handle administrative chores, he quickly became Paley's guide to the new world of journalism in radio.

Paley's other major hire was Paul White. White started his career as a print journalist, working at the *Pittsburg (KS) Headlight*, the *Salina (KS)*

Journal, and the *Kansas City Journal* before leaving the Great Plains for Columbia University, where he earned bachelor's and master's degrees. His specialty was writing simple, direct prose. A former wire-service hand, he was given the chore of running CBS's newsroom. An analysis twenty-five years after his hiring indicated White had succeeded. "Under Mr. White's administration," wrote the *New York Times* at the time of White's death in 1955, "the CBS newsroom gained a reputation as the most competent and alert in radio."[30]

The men hired by CBS during its early days in journalism reflected Paley's orders. One of the new hires was H. V. Kaltenborn. Kaltenborn, a Harvard University graduate fluent in French and German, had worked at the *Brooklyn Eagle*, where he developed a following for his thoughtful analyses of current events. The trend was spreading elsewhere.

NBC, CBS's competitor, gave mixed signals about its commitment to news. NBC bested CBS in its coverage of Edward VII's abdication from the throne in 1936. "NBC's coverage had been better, both before and during the crisis," wrote biographer A. M. Sperber. NBC's superior coverage could be traced directly to Alistair Cooke, who broadcast a half dozen times per day, "a quarter of a million words in the ten-day period," according to Sperber.[31] However, as historian David Holbrook Culbert notes in *News for Everyman*, NBC was not altogether serious about journalism. Culbert writes about Abel A. Schecter, the network's news chief, dreaming up a "singing mice" contest, in which listeners would judge the vocal abilities of the furry creatures. Even as World War II broke out, Schecter seemed unsure about news coverage. When asked about peddling war broadcasts, Schecter responded, "What sponsor would want to sponsor death?"[32]

Another of radio news' early stars was Mutual Broadcasting's Raymond Swing. Swing, like Kaltenborn, was a former print journalist. He started out in the trenches after graduation from Oberlin College as "night man" at the *Cleveland Press*. He worked the "police beat," telephoning Cleveland-area police and fire stations for news and clipping items from other Ohio newspapers for the *Press*'s "State Briefs" column. The training left him with a print journalist's skepticism about the celebrity aspects of the medium, believing that celebrity had a corrosive effect on journalism: "A successful news commentator is, after all, only a journalist magnified by a mechanical device, the microphone. He is not well known for his statesmanship or artistry. He is not creating enduring works. He is not going down in history. But because he is well known, he is constantly tempted to accept as valid the exaggeration some others give to his importance, even though the microphone has not added to his stature or made him wise or and more responsible."[33]

As it turned out, the hiring of Klauber, White, and Mutual's Kaltenborn were propitious moves. A series of international crises escalated into what would become World War II. The crises changed listener attitudes by the late 1930s, according to Kaltenborn. "The intensity with which America listened to the radio reports of the Munich crisis was without parallel in radio history," he later wrote. "People carried them [portable radio sets] to wherever they went, to restaurants, offices, and on the streets. . . . That was the day of taxicab radios and every standing cab was surrounded by crowds as on World Series days. Here was a world series with a vengeance!"[34] Kaltenborn spent hours on the radio analyzing events, employing his German-language skills to translate Adolf Hitler's words and better inform listeners.

As World War II was fought, CBS newsman Edward R. Murrow assembled what was later regarded as one of the finest teams of broadcasters ever gathered. Howard K. Smith was a Rhodes scholar. William L. Shirer had been a noted *Chicago Tribune* correspondent. Murrow liked to say that he had hired these men because of what they knew, not the way they sounded. Shirer had rejected a job offer from the *New York Times* to work for Murrow at CBS. As Shirer later recalled, a former newspaper colleague "couldn't quite believe that a journalist as intelligent as I was would go over to radio, whose handling of the news was superficial and whose public, he said, wanted entertainment, not news." He added: "Murrow had fired me with the feeling that we might go places in the new-fangled radio-broadcasting business. We would have to feel our way. We might find a new dimension for reporting the news. Instantaneous transmission of news from reporter to listener, in his living room (a key speech by Hitler, for example) was utterly new."[35]

The members of Murrow's team, aided by White in New York City, became stars. Murrow was brought back to New York City in midwar for rest and relief. While there, he was feted at an elegant black-tie dinner at one of New York's finest hotels. Archibald Macleish read a poem. "They [the members of the Murrow team] influenced everybody," recalled James F. Clark, who had worked at WWJ-AM and WWJ-FM during the 1940s.

"There wasn't a newsroom in America, from New York to wherever, that wasn't influenced by the Murrow approach to news."[36]

This is not to say that the Murrow team reported the news as a group of dons plucked from among the spires of Oxford. They came across as brave, swashbuckling heroes, and had a certain show business pizzazz about them. Murrow's reportage from atop the rooftops of London during the Blitz made him an idol. Eric Sevareid's exploits during the war similarly made him a heroic figure. He went down in an airplane while traveling between India and China. Lost in the jungles, he came face-to-face with what he thought were headhunters, although it turned out they weren't. When he returned to New York City for a brief stay, a CBS publicist escorted him to a brief audience with Walter Winchell, the quintessential emblem of show business radio. Winchell had little time to meet with Sevareid, but had him guest-write a column. However, the show business flourishes were not the main element for the team. Journalism was.

This traveled back to Detroit in small ways. For example, newscaster Fran Harris's approach to broadcasting the news during the war was more serious than Bradner's, her contemporary. She read the Associated Press, United Press, International News Service, and Reuters dispatches, comparing accounts and making her own best judgment about the day's events. Interested in understanding the world better, she consulted one of her former history professors at Grinnell College about reading material. He suggested the *Christian Science Monitor* and *New York Times*.[37]

After the war ended, WWJ newsroom supervision was taken over by Thomas MacMahon, who, like CBS's White and Klauber, was a print man intent on bringing newspaper standards to radio. A former *Detroit News* editor, MacMahon fashioned himself as the last of the itinerant journalists. Recalled James F. Clark, who worked for MacMahon: "I'd ask him, 'What the hell is an itinerant journalist?' He'd say, 'Tramp reporter. But it sounds better to call myself an itinerant journalist.'" Clark added, "He was a newspaperman. He was out of the old school. It's got to be good. It's got to be succinct. It's got to be well written. And, goddamn it, you're going to do it." Clark noted as well that "being owned by the same company that owned the newspaper, we had to be very careful about our standards. We couldn't exaggerate. We had to be sure what we were talking about."[38]

Not everybody had signed on, however, to the Klauber/White vision of broadcast journalism. There were those who went their own way. One of those was George A. Richards, owner of Detroit's WJR, Los Angeles's KMPC, and Cleveland's WGAR. Richards had owned the Detroit Lions football team between 1934 and 1940. The Federal Communications Commission's chief lawyer asked the FCC to shutter the three stations, arguing that the stations had "not served the public interests."[39] For instance, one Los Angeles newsman recalled receiving instructions from Richards to make former first lady Eleanor Roosevelt appear "drunk." Benedict P. Cottone, the agency's top lawyer, claimed that Richards had used the airwaves for "partisan use."[40]

The case was massive, with the testimony involving KMPC ("the station of the stars") alone involving 3.5 million words and 177 witnesses.[41] One of those who testified in Detroit was Guy Nunn, a former WJR reporter who had lost his job as a result of his coverage of a United Auto Workers' strike against General Motors. As Nunn told a *Detroit Times* reporter: "I watched the pickets from the studio window in the Fisher Building (where WJR's studios were located), read some of the signs over the air and described the scene. I read a statement by the corporation and that was that. Because I couldn't get much from the union for later broadcasts, I later called Walter Reuther at his home or office for a statement. It was two and a half minutes for the company, two and a half minutes for the union. Very fair."[42] Richards did not think so and fired Nunn.

Richards died before the FCC decided the case, and it was eventually dropped. Nunn found work with the United Auto Workers as chief of its radio and television department, going on to become one of the union's best-known public figures.

As for newspapers by the end of the war, CBS News' Paul White wrote: "Listeners realized they were getting the news first by radio, they were getting it condensed, with a minimum of furbishes and foolishness. True, newspapers continued to wax fiscally fat, but the days of powerful influence were gone."[43]

Radio had served itself well with its serious approach. The National Opinion Research Center at the University of Denver asked respondents which medium "did the best job of serving the public during World War II." Radio ranked first, with 67 percent. The new medium far outranked newspapers, which were named by 17 percent of the respondents.[44] Within fifteen years, broadcast journalism evolved from nothing to a respected craft.

The cult of personality in broadcast news was already in place. CBS's White said as much in words written just as television was about to make its debut. Wrote White, describing radio news: "A man gets up at a certain hour because he wants to hear Joe Whoozis give the news. A woman likes to get her housework completed by noon because she then can tune in Vera Velvet, who tells what has been going on in the world."[45]

The key point is that radio news at the time was composed of more journalism than show business. Murrow, the most famous of the World War II–era correspondents, is a case in point. Murrow had faultless instincts for what sounded well on radio. His trademark "This . . . is London," with the brief pause between "This" and "is," gave a dramatic flair to each of his broadcasts. (Murrow had majored in speech at Washington State University.) But Murrow had a concrete belief in the practice of journalism. CBS's William S. Paley supported Murrow in his beliefs. Kaltenborn, Murrow, Swing, and the Murrow team were hailed as great public servants. They were separate from the entertainment traditions of radio.

So when television emerged after World War II, it already had a model to which to aspire. And, as Clark said, Murrow's work had ramifications in every radio newsroom in the United States. That influence was felt in radio newsrooms in Detroit. Radio news had become more serious with the addition of newscasts. The stage was set for the next act. The development of CBS News is one of the odder twists in broadcasting history. "One of the great ironies of CBS is that what started as a public relations ploy by Paley and his aides eventually became one of the most prestigious news organizations in the world," wrote Paley biographer Sally Bedell Smith.[46]

2. TELEVISION

The Early Days

While radio's newsrooms bathed in glory, something was being developed in the CBS and NBC laboratories that would quickly flatten radio's incredible trajectory: television. Television, like radio, began as an entertainment medium. Nowhere was this more evident than in Detroit. Detroit's early stars were a man who took a pie in the face every weekday between noon and 12:30 p.m.; a woman with the improbable but accurate name "Lady of Charm," who dispensed homemaking tips; and a man who became a star showing other people's travel films. Television, for the most part, was not a serious journalistic vehicle. The technological problems were too daunting and the management of the stations too absorbed in the entertainment side of the business for news to be anything more than a headline service. However, the architecture of Detroit television broadcasting would be set. Three companies set up shop in Detroit that would dominate the Detroit airwaves for the next thirty years. The provenance of these companies would govern how and why they did news.

Even as Paul White wrote about the declining influence of newspapers after 1945, the next phase of the communications revolution was well under way. Television had been a pet project of David Sarnoff, chief of the Radio Corporation of America, before World War II. CBS, Sarnoff's network radio rival, was also busy developing plans for the new medium, airing two fifteen-minute news programs each weekday. The station went on the air December 7, 1941, with news of Pearl Harbor. The broadcaster made extensive use of maps, supplemented by expert commentary from Major George Fielding Eliot and Fletcher Pratt. According to one account, "That telecast lasted nine hours. Not more than three or four thousands sets could have been tuned in; but the viewers who did tune in witnessed what was undoubtedly the first TV spectacular—an extended special coverage of a major news event."[1]

A half dozen stations operated during the war, but on a severely limited basis. The Federal Communications Commission ordered a reduction of television broadcasting time from fifteen to four hours per week.

But when World War II ended, broadcasters revisited the development of both radio and television. The FCC did not dawdle in allowing the return to prewar broadcast conditions. The United States dropped an atomic bomb on Hiroshima on August 6, 1945. The next day, even before Japan surrendered, the FCC "removed wartime restrictions for the use of material and equipment for broadcast station construction." The announcement, as might be expected, opened the floodgates. The FCC received as many as one hundred applications for new AM stations a month immediately after World War II.[2] The number of commercial FM stations more than doubled, from 456 to 918 between 1946 and 1947. The number of commercial television stations also doubled, from 30 to 66.[3] The next year showed an even bigger increase, with the number of television stations reaching 109. And that was only part of the picture. Overall, 1,054 new AM stations and 1,061 FM outlets were licensed between VJ Day and mid-1948.[4] But television was where the action was, with Sarnoff's Radio Corporation of America and Paley's CBS each devoting itself to development of the medium.

Television came to a Detroit a little more than a year after VJ Day. The new world of communications in Detroit was born in the attic of the Penobscot Building on October 23, 1946. Gathered atop the city's tallest building, a group of technicians and "talent" employed by Detroit's Evening News Association met to air a three-hour experimental television broadcast. It was easy to tell the pilgrims to this new world; they were the ones with blue makeup. Television's first cameras had problems separating colors. Red did not register. As a result, each of the on-camera personalities was caked in blue makeup. "Blue lips, blue cheeks, and blue eyebrows, an appalling off-camera vision," recalled Fran Harris, who participated in the broadcast.[5] The location of the experimental broadcast, the forty-seventh floor of the Penobscot Building, six blocks from *Detroit News* headquarters, gave a hint as to the chancy nature of the venture. It was out of the way, too. The elevator of the Penobscot Building only went to the forty-fifth floor.

The inaugural program on WWDT, the new station's call letters, lasted three hours. The broadcast provided the best that the Evening News Association had to offer from its radio and newspaper properties, WWJ-AM and the *Detroit News*, respectively. This was "synergy" or "convergence" long before the terms came into wide usage. Dave Zimmerman, host of WWJ-AM's *Coffee Club*, presided over a television edition of the show. In its radio version, the show was performed live with a full band in front of an audience that gathered in an auditorium at WWJ-AM's head-quarters on the west end of downtown Detroit, directly across from the *Detroit News* building. But an audience could not be accommodated in an attic, so Zimmerman did his work without the usual crowd. Tony Weitzel, a popular *Detroit News* columnist who wrote the "Of Cabbages and Kings" column, chatted with his wife. Harris talked with a French chanteuse. An audience gathered at the city's Convention Hall watched on black-and-white monitors.[6] One could call the first broadcast a circus without stretch-ing the term. Rosie the Television Bear made an appearance.

Nor was the *News* alone among newspapers in its interest in the new medium. Newspaper owners had had initial qualms about the radio in-dustry in the 1920s, then embraced radio in a big way. With the debut of television, newspaper owners in search of a new profit center jumped into the new medium at the beginning. Newspaper companies owned at least one-fourth of the television stations, and sometimes as many as two-thirds, during television's first ten years.[7]

The *News* management sensed what it had and wasted no time letting its readers in on its assessment. "Television has an incalculable future," the editors wrote in an edition that appeared within twelve hours of the first broadcast. "Its ultimate possibilities would seem to be bounded only by human imagination. At the moment, its sponsors are like those men of Cortez who stared out into the newfound Pacific with a wild surmise."[8] J. L. Hudson Company officials understood the implications of the new medium. The department store sponsored the broadcast and took out a quarter-page ad in the *News* congratulating the newspaper on the achieve-ment. "The possibilities of television have as yet only been guessed at but its potentialities are most exciting," the ad read.[9] The next day offered another first: "Detroit's first complete television program." Fledgling WWDT aired a Detroit Red Wings hockey game from Olympia, bringing the 6-5 loss to the Chicago Blackhawks live to viewers at Convention Hall. The game featured a goal by rookie Gordon Howe that was called back because of a penalty.[10]

This excitement about the new medium was contagious. Two weeks before Detroit's WWDT broadcast, 1,600 spectators came to the ball-room of New York's Hotel Waldorf-Astoria to view an exhibition by seven manufacturers. One account described the mood of the exhibit as "reminiscent of the early days of radio."[11] Less than two months before the WWDT broadcast, a group of RCA researchers told a gathering of the American Institute of Electrical Engineers that television was ready. "Nothing more is needed, except to do the work of producing in the factories, selling in the stores, and programming in the stations."[12]

Earlier in the year, General Dwight D. Eisenhower had starred in what had been billed as "the first television broadcast from Washington to New York."[13] Eisenhower laid a wreath at the Lincoln Memorial while a television camera broadcast the proceeding. House Speaker Sam Rayburn (D-TX) was there, along with Senator Burton K. Wheeler, chairman of the Interstate Commerce Committee, which would ultimately consider legislation governing this new industry. The reporter characterized their remarks by saying that "legal, social and economic problems remained to be solved before television would come into general use, but they predicted that it would become a boon to mankind." Ralph B. Austrian, general conference chairman of the Television Broadcasters Association, had announced earlier: "The audience at last has assembled, the footlights are on, the orchestra is in the pit, and the curtain is about to rise on the greatest show the world has ever seen. . . . Unlike the great P. T. [Barnum], we're not looking for suckers because, dear public, it's all free."[14] The association's creed was "Uniting All People." In an editorial, *Broadcasting* magazine opined, "The years of hesitation in television—always almost ready for the general public but never quite getting there—are over."[15]

Closer to home, Federal Communications Commission chairman James Coy was quoted in *Broadcasting* as saying, "I foresee the day when television will be the most powerful instrument of communication ever devised, the most universal and most effective purveyor of education, information, culture and entertainment." Author John Steinbeck could not agree with Coy's optimism. He characterized it as a possible "octopus, a monster," but added, "in any event it is the most powerful means of communication ever devised."[16]

Yet there were problems to be solved, wrote *New York Times* critic Jack Gould. He had misgivings about the hoopla and was skeptical about what would later be called "hype." The first television signals had barely wafted into space before Gould wondered if the hucksters promoting the new medium were overselling themselves: "Unrestrained speculation and pre-

diction as to television's implications have been the accepted order, resulting generally in the unqualified conclusion that television is here and
ready now to revolutionize the nation's cultural and entertainment habits."
While conceding that television would be a force at some point, perhaps
soon, Gould still felt the medium faced serious problems. It had barely
begun figuring out how to fill time. He wondered as well about how the
television stations would deal with demands from unions, or even the technical problems involved in sending a picture. "The day unquestionably
will come when television's performance will more than match its present
promise," Gould wrote, "and then video can really blow its own horn. But
that time is not now."[17]

WWJ-TV began broadcasting regularly scheduled programming on
June 3, 1947. The first day of broadcasting included a Detroit Tigers baseball game. The signal went to sets scattered across the city, including the
Book Cadillac Hotel in downtown Detroit. The crowds were so great that
they were broken into two lines to avoid traffic jams. *Detroit News* president William E. Scripps predicted that "political contests of the future will
be of particular interest. For now candidates for public office will have to
look the audience in the eye when making those campaign promises which
in the past have been so glibly tossed at the microphone and which too
often have been forgotten."[18]

WWJ-TV had the field to itself until 1948, when WXYZ-TV and
WJBK-TV went on the air. There were hurdles to overcome, including
the cost of a television set for potential viewers. The television sets adver-
tised in a *Detroit Free Press* special section the day WXYZ-TV went on the
air included a $735 model from Grinnell's; two RCA models, one for $375
and another for $895; a Stromberg-Carlson for $985; a General Electric
for $325; an Emerson for $299.50; and a Magnavox for $345.[19] A television
set during that era represented a hefty investment of household income
by most standards. In 2007 dollars, the aforementioned television sets run
from $2,551.99 to $8,383.02.[20]

Despite the cost of the new appliance, production of television sets
steamed forward. By 1948 television sets were being shipped to Detroit
in bigger numbers. Detroit received 3,933 during the last three months of
1948, about a quarter of the number in Detroit in 1947 and the first nine
months of 1948. Grand Rapids received 16 sets, the rest of Michigan 10.
That was better than other areas of the country. Alabama received only

2 sets in 1947 and the first three quarters of 1948. Nationally, television production levitated to unheard-of figures. Production of television sets in January 1948 had stood at 30,001. By September that number had more than tripled to 95,216, according to the Radio Manufacturers Association. At the same time, AM set production had dropped from 1,173,240 to 869,086.[21]

Factories were turning out television sets, even as broadcasters tentatively felt their way in the new world of communications. By fall 1948 Detroit's television galaxy would take shape. It would include three companies: Detroit's Evening News Association, Toledo's Storer Broadcasting, and New York's American Broadcasting Company. The companies were drastically different in birth, development, and corporate outlook. The Evening News Association, born in nineteenth-century Detroit, remained intimately connected with the city. Storer Broadcasting was a growing broadcast empire based in Toledo, Ohio, with Detroit television only one piece of a larger corporate strategy that involved buying, selling, and trading stations in various markets. The American Broadcasting Company was a fledgling radio and television company that had hoped some day to challenge the much larger and more powerful CBS and NBC networks.

In terms of local impact, the Evening News Association was the most powerful of the three. New York had the Sulzberger and Ochs clan, owners of the *New York Times*. In Los Angeles, the Chandler family controlled the *Los Angeles Times*. In Louisville, the Binghams owned the *Louisville Courier-Journal*. Detroit had the Scripps and Booth families, which had the *Detroit News* and WWJ-AM, one of the city's most powerful radio stations. The families were not unlike the Binghams, the Chandlers, and the Sulzbergers, who influenced their respective cities through their newspapers, the dominant mode of mass communication at the end of the nineteenth century and first quarter of the twentieth century. The families' mark could be seen in many places. George G. Booth, son-in-law of *News* founder James E. Scripps and president of the newspaper between 1906 and 1929, established the Cranbrook Foundation in 1927 with a $20 million donation.[22] Memorializing the death of *News* publisher William E. "Will" Scripps's death in 1952, the *New York Times* described the *News* as "one of the most valuable newspaper properties in the country."[23]

William Scripps, son of *News* founder James Scripps, led the company to experiment with new media. The *News'* WWJ-AM was the first

U.S. radio station in 1920 to air regularly scheduled programs, although Westinghouse's KDKA-AM in Pittsburgh made a similar claim. In Detroit, the Evening News Association held major stakes in both electronic and print information. Readers and listeners could not miss the connection if they tried. The newspaper's masthead proudly reminded readers that James E. Scripps had founded the newspaper on August 23, 1873. It also informed readers that the company had established WWJ on August 28, 1920, and founded FM station WENA on May 9, 1941. WENA, of course, stood for Evening News Association. If the *Chicago Tribune*'s Colonel Robert McCormick could name his radio station WGN so listeners would remember the *Chicago Tribune* and its trademark "World's Greatest Newspaper," Detroit listeners similarly would remember who owned Detroit's biggest newspaper. WWJ listeners were also reminded each time the station identified itself with the line "This is WWJ, the *Detroit News*." And when curious viewers showed up to watch television's first broadcast at Detroit's Convention Hall, they were again reminded. The big, boxlike cameras carried a "WWDT *Detroit News*" sign.

The Scripps family foray into television was a natural. The family was a family of tinkerers, interested in the latest technology. Will Scripps was believed to have been the first Michigan man to both fly and own an airplane, according to an official *News* biography. One of the finest radio receivers and transmitters stood in the Scripps home on Trumbull Avenue near Grand River.[24] During the late 1940s and early 1950s, he could often be found puttering in the *News* garage. Although the question of whether WWJ-AM was the oldest radio station in the country was in dispute, the *News* was clearly the first newspaper in the country to own a radio station. And the new television station was a first in Michigan.

The story was the same in many other places. The owners of the *St. Louis Post-Dispatch* were remodeling the newspaper's building to incorporate a television studio.[25] The list of newspaper companies petitioning for television licenses or construction permits as of late September 1946 included some of the era's greatest newspaper corporations (see appendix, table 3).

There were others on the FCC docket. The Times-Mirror Company, owner of the powerful *Los Angeles Times*, had a television application pending, as did WGN, Inc., which was owned by the *Chicago Tribune*.[26] Within two years there would be many others. The *Atlanta Journal* would enter the television world with WSB-TV. Newspaper/television cross-owner-ship was becoming quite common. On election night in 1948, WTMJ-TV broadcast from the *Milwaukee Journal* Building, WBZ-TV from the *Boston Globe*, and WMAR-TV showed how its owners, the A. S. Abell Company, printed the *Baltimore Sun*.[27] In each case, the broadcaster was primarily a newspaper company.

Unlike the Evening News Association, the American Broadcasting Company had no roots in Detroit or in print journalism. The company had purchased WXYZ-TV and WOOD-TV in Grand Rapids for $3.65 mil-lion, backed by a stock issue of 1 million shares, while also buying stations in Los Angeles, San Francisco, New York, and Chicago.[28] In landing WXYZ, ABC became owner of one of the most storied local stations in the history of broadcasting. WXYZ had created the *Lone Ranger*, the *Green Hornet*, and *Sgt. Preston*. But it was the television station that drew ABC's interest.

The American Broadcasting Company was born by court order. After an exhaustive investigation during the late 1930s and early 1940s into media ownership, the Federal Communications Commission ordered the National Broadcasting Company to divest itself of one of its two radio networks. NBC chose to unload the NBC Blue Network, selling it to businessman Edward J. Noble for $8 million. The newly born American Broadcasting Company quickly ran into financial difficulties. "By 1951, Noble was almost desperate to sell ABC," recalled Leonard Goldenson, who later went on to become chairman of the ABC board. "After buying another radio station, WXYZ Detroit, and building five television stations, the company was losing money."[29] Noble sold ABC to United Paramount Theatres, Inc. for $25 million. But even then, the FCC was reluctant to approve the merger, studying the proposed deal before finally approving the sale in February 1953.

The new network was dwarfed by NBC and CBS, both in financial re-sources and in number of affiliates. At the time of the merger, ABC's affiliate television lineup stood at fourteen stations, roughly one-fifth the number claimed each by NBC and CBS. Profits from ABC's five owned stations dur-ing television's early days were crucial to the company's operation. Tables 4 through 7 (see appendix) illustrate how NBC and CBS overwhelmed ABC during the early to mid-1950s, and the importance of its five stations. As table 4 illustrates, the ABC Television Network lost money in 1953 and 1954 but made a slight profit in 1955. Such was the precariousness of ABC's financial position that it lost more money in 1952 than DuMont, a fledgling network that would fold September 15, 1955. In contrast, ABC's stations' division made profits in each of the years between 1953 and 1955, and was responsible for the bulk of ABC's $5.6 million earnings in 1955.

The other factor was heritage. NBC and CBS each had a legacy dating back to the days of radio. ABC had no such broadcast lineage. And while NBC News and CBS News had distinguished themselves with their war coverage, ABC could make no such claim. It was a company feeling its way, both in television and in the booming world of broadcasting.

All of the networks depended on local affiliates to carry their program. In Detroit, CBS relied on Storer Broadcasting's WJBK-TV. The station was the creation of George B. Storer, a Toledo businessman with two decades of broadcasting experience. Storer entered the Detroit television market, buying the license for WJBK in 1947 from businessmen James F. Hopkins and Richard A. Connell for $550,000.[30] At the same time he applied for television licenses in Miami and Toledo.[31] Building three television stations simultaneously was considered a gamble, given the untried nature of the new medium.

Storer began his business career in the steel and gas industries. He had been a student at Cornell University when he inherited his father's job as president of Standard Steel and Tube Company in Toledo, Ohio. Storer later branched into the gasoline business, founding Fort Industry Oil Company, whose "purpose was to save money on distribution costs by putting gas stations next to railroad sidings so gas could be sold more cheaply," wrote John Floyd Wellman in a study of the corporation.[32] The cornerstone of what would become the Storer Broadcasting empire was set with Toledo's WTOL, which Storer bought in 1927 for $3,500. He soon discovered that radio was an effective advertising medium. By the time he founded WJBK-TV in Detroit, he had already made two forays into Detroit broadcasting. He had owned WGHP-AM, the station that later became WXYZ-AM, between 1920 and 1930. He also built CKLW-AM in 1930, but sold it one year later.[33] In addition, Storer owned stations in Wheeling, West Virginia; Fairmont, Ohio; Lima, Ohio; Zanesville, Ohio; and Miami, Florida.

Storer already had something of a reputation as a well-connected operator by the time WJBK-TV went on the air. Storer's brother-in-law and business partner, J. Harold Ryan, had been president of the National Association of Broadcasters.[34] Only four years before, Storer and James

Lawrence Fly, chairman of the Federal Communications Commission, were connected in a federal investigation. Ralph A. Horton, owner of WTFL in Ft. Lauderdale, Florida, had been in negotiations to sell the station to Storer. John J. Sirica, a lawyer for a Special House Committee investigating the FCC, presented evidence that, according to one account, gave Horton "the impressions that the financial set-up of the Horton station was in conflict with the Communications Act and might be put off the air."[35] Fly met with Horton in Atlanta and, according to Horton, implied that Horton might have FCC problems if he did not sell the station to Storer. Horton sold WTFL for $275,000, an estimated $225,000 under its potential market value. Fly denied the plot and the story faded. But Storer's reputation as a well-connected dealer did not.

By 1948 the players were in place—the Evening News Association, Storer Broadcasting, and the American Broadcasting Company. The second phase of Detroit television development began in earnest with the debut of WXYZ-TV on October 9, 1948.[36] WXYZ-TV's inaugural broadcast was loaded with sports, including a World Series baseball game between the Cleveland Indians and Boston Braves, part of a football game between the University of Michigan and Notre Dame, a sportscast by Don Wattrick, who had also worked at WXYZ radio, and a Detroit Lions football game, live from Briggs Stadium.[37] Storer threw the switch at WJBK-TV October 24, 1948, airing CBS and DuMont programs.[38]

Now that three broadcasters had managed to put their stations on the air, Gould's 1946 prediction turned out to be correct in another way. Once the problem of putting a signal up was solved, filling time became an even greater problem.

The act of broadcasting a program could be uncomfortable. "The plastic tile floor just curled up and died and had to be replaced immediately. If you were 'on-camera' for as little as 10 minutes, those 800–1000-foot-candle overhead lights guaranteed not only bright red skin, but also little wisps of steam rising from every pore," recalled Sonny Eliot, who performed in numerous WWJ-TV shows in the late 1940s. "You could certainly part your hair in the middle and irrigate your eyebrows. Back then we didn't reckon with TV's great influence, and hardly realized how it would change our lives. It was just something new, exciting and experimental. You learned on the job."[39] Ron David began as a producer and director at WXYZ-TV, not long after the station went on the air. For him,

Every day was an adventure. Everything was live. There was very little or no rehearsal of anything. At Channel 7, all of the directors and stage managers had five or six shows a day. We'd work all day doing television. After work, we'd go to the Alcove Bar, right next to the Maccabees Building [where Channel 7's studios were headquartered]. It was a Damon Runyon bar. You had a combination of hookers, pimps and murderers all mixed in with the TV folks.

We would try things. We'd do things like take a Dixie cup, paint the inside of it black and poke a hole in the bottom with a pencil. We'd put that paper cup over the lens and put somebody's head over a hole so we could super-impose the picture on the screen. That's how crude things were. Sometimes it worked. Sometimes it didn't. The fun part was that if you screwed up, everybody saw it.

It was just a ball, one happy family. When I first started I was seventeen. I went to Wayne [State University] full time, and I was so eager to learn. All of the engineers there were really tough. I would beg them to let me run a camera. And they did. We would back each other up. It was fresh and new in those days. Nobody got paid a lot of money. As a matter of fact, I think I was making $50 a week, as a director, maybe $100–$200 a week. But we thought that was big money. The whole spirit of camaraderie was there, because we knew we needed each other badly, and we were trying to figure out this new animal called television.

I sat down in a chair at 10:30 at night. I did a 15-minute weathercast back-to-back with 15 minutes of "Deadline Detroit," back to back with "Soupy's On," back to back with "Night Court." I'd get out of the chair at 12:30 at night. And every single bit was live. We were young. We could take it. We loved what we were doing. We'd sign the station off, go to the Alcove Bar, drink until daylight, go home for a couple hours sleep, and come back for more.[40]

David's colleagues were mostly young, energetic Detroiters who couldn't believe their good fortune to be working in the new medium. One was Mort Zieve, who produced and/or directed many of Channel 7's programs. He was a Detroit native, a graduate of Detroit's Central High School and Wayne State University. Zieve also earned a master's degree from Stanford University, hoping to become a theater director. He spent time starving in New York City working toward his goal. When an opportunity opened up at WXYZ-TV, he took it. Zieve, who was born in 1927, hadn't yet turned thirty and was already producing or directing some of the most distinctive shows on Detroit TV, including *Auntie Dee*, Soupy Sales's nighttime program, and *Lady of Charm*.[41] Zieve prided himself on doing a lot with a little and reveled in the creative process. One classic story involved Zieve in a spirited argument with a competing WWJ-TV producer. The Channel 4 producer told Zieve: "You guys take shit and turn it into money." Zieve replied: "You guys take money and turn it into shit." Another anecdote illustrates the family atmosphere at ABC and the respect garnered by Zieve. In the late 1950s, Zieve had thoughts of trying his luck in New York City. ABC chairman Leonard Goldenson wrote an enthusiastic letter on Zieve's behalf but had some fatherly advice: moving a wife and child to New York in hopes of getting a job would be difficult. (Zieve would leave Channel 7 in 1961 for a job in advertising. He later became chairman of the board of the Simons Michelson Zieve (SMZ) ad agency, which handled a list of blue-chip clients, including the Big Boy restaurants, Michigan Lottery, Midas Mufflers, Cunningham Drug Stores, and the Detroit Tigers.)

The new medium concentrated heavily on entertainment programming. News was not taken seriously at first. During the summer of 1950, for instance, WJBK-TV offered a fifteen-minute newscast, *5-Star Final News*, between 10:00 and 10:15 p.m., followed by fifteen minutes of sports.[42] WXYZ-TV offered the five-minute program *News of the Day* between 10:25 and 10:30 p.m. As at WJBK-TV, WXYZ-TV's sportscast was twice as long as its newscast: *Baseball Scorecard* ran ten minutes nightly, sometimes between 11:00 and 11:10 p.m., sometimes between 10:50 and 11:00 p.m. News, weather, and sports each had separate time periods, sponsors, theme music, and openings and closings. The sponsors were much in evidence; WJBK-TV's Jac Le Goff, for instance, wore sponsor Standard Oil's patch on his suit jacket.

Newscasts in Detroit during the earliest decade of television were relatively simple, as James F. Clark explained:

At first, we patterned our copy and patterned our presentation pretty much as an afterthought of radio, like applying radio to a new medium, because at first we had to rely on film instead of videotape. We had to use a lot of still pictures [of newsmakers] and things like that. Things were directed toward more of an audio presentation than directed toward a visual presentation. Nowadays, everything is visual. In those days, the audio presentation was foremost. The visual was more of an afterthought, the beginning of a new medium, although fires were big. Many times, when we'd look at the kinescopes, we'd say, "This is a radio newscast being presented on television." That was our own reaction.[43]

Reporters or anchormen would often use still photographs, often borrowed from Detroit's newspapers, to illustrate stories. Sid Siegal, an early WJBK-TV cameraman, thought he had a way of improving that system. During the 1940s, the process of developing film could take as long as a week. Siegal devised a system that would require less than a day. He thought he would get somewhere pitching the idea to Detroit's TV stations. "The news departments had no film. They were using AP wirephotos. There was no film whatsoever. Once in awhile, they would get something that might be a week old," he recalls. Siegal got nowhere with his presentation. "[It was] totally not received at all. The idea was 'Who needs it? We're getting along fine.' I can buy a feature film for Hollywood for five bucks. Why the hell should I spend several hundred dollars a week on news film?"[44]

His efforts went unnoticed until 1952, when a story of stranded GIs hit the newspapers. They had received their discharge but had no way of getting home. A sympathetic public and a group of industrialists paid for their trip home. Siegal filmed their arrival in Detroit:

I was there with my sixteen-millimeter camera and took it back to my closet—so to speak; it was a closet, really—to develop the film. I took it down to Channel 2. I didn't show it to them. I just told them what I had. They said, "Can we run it on the air?" I said "Sure." It was uncut, unedited. But it was a news story. The next day there was a blizzard. So I filmed the blizzard and delivered the news to the station. The third day there was cleanup after the blizzard. I did the same thing. I did that for five days in a row, to prove that I could deliver. My own camera, my own film, my own processing. . . . The news department had no film. . . . On the fifth day they said go see Dick Jones, the station manager. He sat there in a cloud of smoke and said: "OK smart ass, how much do you want?" I named a figure. I was paid $350 a week. I supplied everything: film, car, processing and—when needed—a soundman.[45]

Those who were involved in newsrooms of the day say that content in the 1950s was not unlike the content of the current day. "That much hasn't changed," says WWJ-TV's Eliot. "You'd have freeway accidents, fires, animal and children stories, the same sort of thing you see today."[46] What film there was sometimes came from Movietone, a visual service provided to television stations by United Press. By today's standards, newscast delivery was stiff, dull, and newspaperlike. Except for WWJ-TV's Sonny Eliot, broadcasters rarely interjected personality. Independent reporting was rare, too. Newscasters relied heavily on the Associated Press and United Press International wires. WJBK-TV anchorman Jac Le Goff recalled that a newscast at his station was a two-person effort, involving the anchorman and the cameraman, leaving little time for independent newsgathering.

> We had one cameraman, Murray Young. Murray—he produced, he filmed, he edited, he did everything when it came to film. He produced a complete package, from the opening frame to the close, which included the voice-over material as well as whatever sound bites he might be able to get—although at that time he had a budget of $25 a week for a sound engineer, if you can believe that. . . . We did it all ourselves—we meaning John Kelly and me, when we were working together for a number of years. Before the advent of John Kelly, I did it myself. It was almost a case of rip and read, because there just wasn't time to put everything together that had to be put together for a given newscast—particularly the 11:00. . . . We kind of had to fly by the seat of our pants. The national news—we had to wait until the last plane came in from New York, which was generally around 10:00. We knew what the content was going to be, but we had no idea of what the picture itself was going to be like. . . . We never had the chance to screen it. We put it on the air cold. . . . Murray had his own lab. He processed his own film. That was his full-time job: not just a photographer, but the film processor as well. It was a two-man deal.

When asked why management did not hire others, Le Goff recalled, "It was a reluctance on their part to invest the kind of money that it took to come up with a first-class operation."[47]

Fran Harris, writing about the early days of television, described the early attitude about news from most managers.

Television news wasn't popular in those years [the late 1940s] either. It was considered dull, hard to sell, and a nuisance to the sales department. World War II was over and it was thought that people preferred entertainment. Besides, good reporters were hard to find. They worked for the big newspapers and magazines and wouldn't deign to appear on TV, so the early newscasters of the late '40s and early '50s were announcers who simply read what was put before them. Radio had newscasts, so television did too, but the news items were limited to those coming over the teletype and from the *Detroit News* desks. After all, for TV to cover news well meant going where the news was, which meant acquiring better remote equipment and more manpower. It was too iffy and too costly.[48]

David Brinkley put it just as succinctly. News, at first, simply was not on the radar screen of the typical broadcast executive. Wrote Brinkley, "The broadcast management community usually sees a news program as a nice thing to do, an effort they probably ought to make and money they probably ought to spend, but not really their reason for existence. Their reason for existence lies elsewhere, in entertainment and advertising, not in journalism."[49]

Resources at WXYZ-TV were even worse. The station dropped news during the last half of the 1950s to run *Soupy's On*, featuring children's star Soupy Sales, who popularized on television the comedic device of being hit in the face with a pie. "I think John Pival [WXYZ-TV's general manager] figured he'd make more money from pies than from news," surmised Dave Diles, who was hired in 1960 as a sportscaster.[50] "News did not interest John Pival," wrote Dick Osgood, who worked at the station as a news announcer and show host. He described the station's fledgling news operation, which was run by Dick Femmel.

It was some time before Pival would let Femmel hire a full-time photographer. WXYZ's first full-time movie cameraman for news was a square-dance enthusiast, with white hair and spectacles, Art Mazur. If a story was important enough, Femmel might go out with him, but usually Dick told him where to go and what to capture in his camera. Mazur would stop on his way back to have the film developed by a man who had a lab in his basement and could develop in a hurry. His chemicals were not always fresh which created problems. It was a crude operation.

Osgood quoted Femmel as saying, "We never had a budget to do anything. It was always clinging to news by your fingernails."[51] WXYZ-TV's five-minute newscasts in the 1950s were "rip and read" affairs, with an announcer simply presenting a short block of news. (Even after Sales left for California in early 1961, WXYZ-TV still did not jump into news. In 1961, for instance, the station ran *Racket Squad*, *Mr. and Mrs. North*, *Girl Decoy*, *Mickey Spillane*, and *State Trooper* during the 11:00 p.m. time period.)[52]

It was not that WXYZ-TV could not afford a news department. The station, which was making enormous amounts of money for ABC, found it more lucrative to stay with entertainment programming. A congressional subcommittee looking into the television industry released WXYZ-TV's balance sheet in 1957. It showed that the station was the second most profitable among ABC's five stations, at least twice as profitable as ABC's outlets in the bigger cities of New York and Los Angeles (see appendix, tables 8–10).

As the tables illustrate, ABC invested less in Detroit during the years between 1953 and 1955 than any of its other four television properties. ABC, in fact, was using its Detroit and Chicago stations to, among other things, finance building in the bigger markets of New York City and Los Angeles in 1953.

Still, the Detroit public during the early 1950s had an appetite for televised public events. The Senate Crime Committee, generally known as the Kefauver Committee, traveled to Detroit in February 1951 to investigate organized crime in the city.[53] WWJ-TV and WJBK-TV aired the proceedings, which summoned a wild public response. According to *Broadcasting/Telecasting*:

Detroiters, through the eyes and ears of TV . . . were able to attend a real-life whodunit when the U.S. Senate Crime Investigating Committee held hearings in the Motor City last fortnight.

Public reaction to the two-day hearings was reportedly unprecedented. Thousands of letters and phone calls from Detroit residents inundated the studios of WWJ-TV and WJBK-TV thanking the stations for their part in exposing the face of evil.

Nearly every other activity paused as televiewers riveted themselves before an estimated 90 percent of the city's screens to watch hoodlums squirm under the relentless questioning of the committee.

Door-to-door salesmen were unable to tear housewives away from telecasts and retreated into bars themselves to watch. As one bartender commented in a letter to WJBK-TV: "The place was crowded all day. They didn't drink much, but that's OK with me." The bartender himself was absorbed in the hearings.[54]

The airing of the crime committee hearings would have been in character for WWJ-TV as it moved away from the attitude described earlier by Harris. The station's corporate owners, the Evening News Association, invested money in its news operation. Exactly how much is difficult to determine, because the Evening News Association was not a publicly held corporation and did not file annual reports. The investment benefited all corners of the association's Detroit media empire. Newscasters usually worked both on WWJ-AM and WWJ-TV, increasing cross-promotional opportunities. News director Jim Clark increased his budget requests most years during the 1950s, asking for money for another crew or two. Usually his requests were granted. "Each year I would ask for more money," Clark later noted, "and each year the senior officers would ask, 'Why do you need more?' And I would simply say, 'This is what it takes.'"[55]

Clark had another advantage. The WWJ-TV's news operation had access to the *Detroit News* newsroom. Duplicate copies of *News* stories were routinely sent from the *News* building across the street to WWJ-TV studios. The staffs mingled at lunch at the *News* cafeteria. At night the staffs gathered at the Adams Bar, located immediately next to WWJ-TV and across the street from the *News* building. A tunnel that ran beneath West Lafayette Boulevard connected the two operations.

Clark created a "beat" system so reporters could develop expertise in their assigned areas. Most television stations (then as well as now) moved journalists randomly from one story to the next, "like paratroopers—they'd jump into a story and jump out." Instead, Clark assigned reporters to single topics, so they could develop an expertise and report more intelligently. Clark remembered later the reason he forced the change: "Unfortunately, television reporters had to be very, very shallow—jack of all trades—do a little bit of this, a little bit of that. It bugged me because they didn't research stories as they should be researched." In Clark's new system Kirk Knight, for instance, covered the Detroit Common Council. Ven Marshall became an expert on the Teamsters and labor. Britt Temby reported on the United Auto Workers.[56]

He also forced reporters to become writers. Clark said he "was proud of our guys, because they not only developed their own stories, they had to do their own writing. As a result, they were very knowledgeable. . . . I thought that what we did was put a little integrity in the television news business. I could see the way it was going—and it has developed into what I was afraid it was going to—a lack of integrity."[57]

The result: credibility—not only in the journalism world but among viewers. "What he did was assemble the first credible local broadcast news operation in the country," said Bill Bonds, who tried without success to get Clark to hire him for his first TV job.[58]

One who saw the difference between the WWJ-TV operation and the others was Carl Cederberg, who'd worked at WWJ-TV and WWJ-AM beginning in 1955, then left to join WJBK-TV in 1960. When Cederberg signed on at WJBK-TV, the news department consisted of a part-time news director and a photographer. That was it. Cederberg was shocked at the meager conditions of the news departments and the nightly scramble to Metropolitan Airport for CBS film. He had a hard time believing it.[59]

The best measure of how seriously local television took news can be illustrated by how much time was spent broadcasting news. While part of the Detroit daily television schedule, journalism was overshadowed by entertainment. Tables 11 through 13 (see appendix) show a breakdown of time devoted to news in sample dates from 1950 to 1959.

As evidenced by the three tables, commitment to news varied widely. Placing the charts in context, the broadcast day of Detroit's television stations expanded during the early 1950s. In 1950, for instance, the three stations signed on between 2:00 p.m. and 3:00 p.m., and signed off at approximately 11 p.m. The broadcast day had expanded by 1952, with each of the stations signing on at approximately 7:00 a.m. or 7:30 a.m., and then running until about midnight.

As the charts illustrate, WXYZ-TV avoided news, dropping to as little as five minutes daily during the 1950s. The station's news time during the early 1950s, when it devoted as much as forty minutes daily to news, is somewhat misleading. Many of the newscasts were aired in five-minute increments, with an announcer simply reading headlines. Most newscasts ran fifteen minutes, which was the norm at the television network divisions.

WWJ-TV would use five minutes of time allotted by NBC's *Today* for local news. In addition, both WJBK-TV and WWJ-TV borrowed formats from the radio schedule. This would include fifteen-minute newscasts at 6:00 p.m. and 11:00 p.m., which had become a staple of radio. It also included running a ten-minute sportscast and a five-minute weathercast separately after the news. Each of the three programs had its own sponsor and its own structure of a beginning, middle, and end.

WWJ-TV and WJBK-TV made an attempt at news, performing to the standards of the day. CBS News and NBC News each ran fifteen-minute newscasts during the 1950s, as did many local television stations. WXYZ-TV made little attempt to meet those standards. As we shall see later, the station could not claim lack of resources.

The people delivering those fifteen-minute newscasts on early Detroit television were drawn from the ranks of radio, not newspapers or the wire services, which had become Edward R. Murrow's choice for hiring. Most were born and educated in the Midwest and had worked in radio as announcers or reporters before entering television. Print experience was rare. What follows are the backgrounds of the earliest television reporters and news chiefs.

WWJ's James F. Clark was arguably the most influential Detroit television news executive during the 1950s. Clark ran the station's news department between 1953 and 1970, and also anchored the news for a short time at WWJ-TV. Clark began his broadcasting career as an announcer on WENA-FM, which was considered the boondocks of radio. After serving in the military during World War II, he returned to work as an announcer on WWJ-AM. Clark watched Detroit's first television broadcast as it was put on the air in 1947. "It was more of a novelty at first," he later recalled. "Nobody could really comprehend the impact that television was going to make on our society."[60]

Clark rode herd over a stable of reporters, almost all of whom had worked in radio. Kirk Knight was among WWJ-TV's first hires. Knight had worked as a radio newsman in Detroit since 1929 before beginning a career in the new television medium at the age of forty. His duties included local news "cut-ins" during the NBC's *Today Show* between 1952 and 1973.

Paul Williams, Knight's contemporary, was even more widely seen. Williams, who is said to be Detroit's first full-time anchorman, was also

Detroit's original sportscaster. He anchored Detroit's first newscast in 1947 and also called Detroit Tigers, Detroit Lions, Detroit Red Wings, and University of Michigan football games.

Williams began his career in Detroit as a sportscaster. He joined Ty Tyson in the broadcast booth for University of Michigan football games, and served as a Detroit Tigers television sportscaster between 1947 and 1952. Williams served as a newscaster from 1952 to 1962, continuing on as the station's public affair's manager for a dozen years after that. His colleagues remembered him as a man of grit—a man who, when struck by a heart attack during a newscast, remained on the set until the conclusion of the broadcast.[61]

A staff of on-air reporters backed Williams. One of the first to be hired was Carl Cederberg, who was added to the staff in 1955. Like Knight and many of his television news contemporaries, Cederberg was a radioman from the Midwest. A Bay City native, Cederberg got his first taste of broadcasting as a high school student working part-time at a Bay City/Saginaw radio station. He remembers delivering war news to his fellow students over the public address system after Pearl Harbor. Cederberg continued his youthful career as a war correspondent by signing on at Armed Forces Radio Services during World War II. He worked as a newscaster in Milne Bay, New Guinea.

Cederberg's hiring at WWJ-AM was a rare case of being in the right place at the right time—literally. "I stopped by the station to see the studios, because I'd heard they were state-of-the-art," he later recalled. "But the receptionist told me they didn't give tours, and the only way for me to see the equipment was to come in and audition."[62] Cederberg did just that, and was given a job. In addition to anchoring key radio newscasts, Cederberg worked on WWJ-TV's early television news endeavors.

Reporter Ven Marshall was hired within a year of Cederberg and covered some of Detroit's biggest political and labor stories from the 1950s until the 1980s. Marshall's strength was his broad range of sources. "If he had been covering the Titanic," colleague Bill Bonds recalled, "he would have a guy on the iceberg with a cell phone waiting to call Ven when it happened."[63] One could say that a few of Marshall's sources were a family affair. His brother, Bill, was a longtime head of the metropolitan Detroit AFL-CIO.

Marshall's dramatic baritone carried shades of Edward R. Murrow. He had worked in Flint radio before signing on at WWJ-TV in 1956. "Ven had a vinyl disc recording of his work during the Flint tornado," remembered WWJ-TV's Jim Clark. "He did really outstanding work on the Flint tornado."[64] The outstanding work continued in Detroit. Colleague Dwayne X. Riley described Marshall's commitment to his craft:

He was intense, a buzz saw. In those days, when he was anchoring the news on weekends, it was a simple operation. There would be one crew—and that would be it. They didn't go out unless something really big happened. We didn't have producer upon producer, assistant producers, writers and the rest. He would do it all. He'd mat these photographs, run across the room to answer the telephone, write something, and run back to the photo machine for more photographs. It was amazing to see. All of it was way beyond the call of duty. But that was Ven—extraordinarily conscientious.[65]

Probably the station's most familiar face was Dick Westerkamp, who anchored WWJ-TV's newscasts between 1956 and 1968. Standing behind a podium, he began each broadcast with the phrase "Good evening, I'm Dick Westerkamp. The temperature in Detroit is ——." Westerkamp was Detroit's most-watched newscaster throughout most of the 1950s and 1960s. He began his journalism career as a newsman in Ashland, Kentucky, and Buffalo, New York. Colleagues recall Westerkamp's work ethic. "He'd check every fact, question everybody about what they knew. Nothing got by him," recalled Ken Hissong, who worked in the newsroom during that era.[66]

His delivery was unemotional and direct. "He had what I called the 'Ed Sullivan charm,'" said Sonny Eliot, who worked alongside him during Westerkamp's entire Detroit career. "He couldn't read a funny story to save his life, and he'd screw up. People would see this and say, 'Heck, I can do better than that,' which is the same thing they said about Sullivan. But, as with Sullivan, they watched. Westerkamp had a sincerity that people believed in."[67] WWJ-TV news director Jim Clark thought that Westerkamp had a connection with viewers. "I think it was his down-to-earth presentation. He'd come on many times and fluff his own name at the beginning. . . . I think that people just learned to like the guy, because he had a straightforward way of presenting the news. . . . I think sometimes they'd watch to see if he could get through a story alright."[68]

The man who possibly had more influence than anybody was a man unknown to viewers. He was E. L. (Hank) Shurmur, who either shot or developed virtually every piece of film seen on WWJ-TV during the 1950s and 1960s. Channel 4 had no photographers of its own. Instead, the station subcontracted the chores out to Shurmur's company, NLU Productions—which stood for "Never Let 'Em Up." (Another of his companies was the "We Never Sleep" Newsreel Service. The monikers summarized Shurmur's journalistic philosophy.) WWJ-TV hired Shurmer's company, Shurmur, in turn, hired his own people as subcontractors. His company processed every inch of film broadcast over WWJ-TV's airwaves well into the 1970s. Shurmur was one of the most distinctive "characters" in post–World War II journalism. Shurmur and *Detroit News* columnist Doc Greene were close friends and enthusiastic habitués of downtown Detroit's watering holes. He would open many conversations with the phrase "Lissen, you sonofabitch . . ." as in "Lissen, you sonofabitch, I had the best steak last night." "He never meant anything by that," recollected Dwayne X. Riley, a Shurmur contemporary. "That was just the way he talked." Shurmur also ran the "Ecclesiastical Shakedown Society," which raised tens of thousands of dollars for downtown Detroit's Holy Trinity Church and which served a poor neighborhood just west of downtown Detroit. Nobody was exempt from Shurmur's arm—including Bishop Fulton J. Sheen, who contributed $100 to the group after getting the Shurmur treatment.[69]

Shurmur began his career as a public relations man and newsreel photographer, filming General George Patton's troops as they crossed the Rhine River during World War II. He had numerous jobs after the war, including handling bookings for bowler Andy Varipapa.

Shurmur's range of acquaintances was varied and legendary—from downtown Detroit bartenders to the presidents of the major auto companies. They'd show up at Shurmur's parties—dubbed "Slug Your Buddy" bashes because fistfights had a way of breaking out during the course of the evening. He was connected with Teamster president Jimmy Hoffa, who hired him to film Teamster conventions. Shurmur once had a drink with President Harry Truman. Not long before Shurmur died, his friends threw a party for him at Detroit's Cobo Hall, the only place that could contain Shurmur's vast array of pals. Attendees included United Auto

Workers president Walter Reuther, two future UAW presidents (Leonard Woodcock and Doug Fraser), Detroit mayor Roman S. Gribbs, and a past mayor (Jerome P. Cavanagh). A half dozen judges and two congressmen were listed as cosponsors. New York mayor Robert Wagner, a close friend of Shurmur's from his war days, delivered one of the speeches.[70]

"Uneducated and obscene of speech, he never really realized what a good man he had become," the late Doc Greene wrote on the occasion of Shurmur's death. "Some of us did."[71]

For on-air work, WJBK-TV leaned heavily on former radio reporters. Ken Cline was among the department's first hires. Cline first signed on as WJBK-AM's news director in 1948, the same year WJBK-TV went on the air. He transferred to Storer's new TV station within the year, later anchoring the news on weekends throughout the 1950s and 1960s.

In a departure from normal hiring traditions, WJBK-TV hired two intellectuals during the 1950s. One of them was Dr. Everett Phelps, the station's meteorologist between 1951 and 1958. Phelps began working in television during its infancy. He was WXYZ-TV's "Mr. Weather" in 1950, two years after the station went on the air. Despite Phelps's moniker, he had an impressive list of credentials: holder of a PhD in physics from the University of Michigan, he cowrote a textbook, *Practical Shop Mathematics*, which was translated into Italian. Considered a classic, the book was still used three decades after his death. In addition to Phelps's television appearances, he had also worked since 1922 as a professor of physics and astronomy at Wayne State University.

Phelps believed his background "enabled me to give a weather program in a manner which makes it more understandable to the average viewer."[72] When the Soviet Union launched the Sputnik in 1959, Phelps expertly showed viewers where and when to watch the spacecraft as it passed through the skies of Detroit. Or, after Christmas, he would show the new owners of barometers (figuring the barometers had shown up as holiday gifts) how to adjust the new instruments to sea level.

Dr. John Dempsey was the other academic serving on the WJBK-TV staff. Dempsey earned his PhD in political science from the University of Michigan in 1956, joining WJBK-TV the same year. He wore two hats at the television station, working as a commentator and also supervising WJBK-TV's news department. He returned to academia a half dozen years later, joining the University of Michigan–Dearborn, where he taught until 1969.

Anchorman Jac Le Goff outlasted all of them, anchoring newscasts in Detroit into the 1990s. Le Goff had joined WJBK-TV in 1953 as an anchorman, becoming the station's news director. He was also, as far as can be determined, the only Detroit television news figure to be written about on the front page of any of Detroit's three major newspapers during the 1950s. A scandal in rock music radio involving payola, the illicit practice of taking money to play recordings during a program, surfaced in Detroit and nationwide in 1959. Although the scandal involved the competing medium of radio, all three Detroit television stations had sister radio stations. Storer Broadcasting Company owned WJBK-TV and WJBK-AM, The American Broadcasting Company owned WXYZ-TV and WXYZ-AM, and the Evening News Association owned WWJ-TV, WWJ-AM, and WWJ-FM. Three radio hosts lost their jobs before the scandal was over. WJBK-AM's Tom Clay admitted taking money and was fired. Dale Young, his colleague, did not admit taking money but resigned one day after Clay's dismissal. WXYZ-AM's Mickey Shorr had a financial involvement with a record company. Station officials saw that as a conflict of interest and fired him.

Le Goff lost his job as well, but not because of any illegal activity. Detroit's newspapers ran front-page stories about the radio imbroglio for three days when Le Goff, without any warning to station management, delivered the following editorial:

WJBK has received a number of calls from listeners today asking why we didn't carry the story concerning the disc jockeys of radio and the story about payola, or bribery, to play a certain record.

I didn't use the story at 11 last night, realizing that the newspapers would hop on this as they did on the so-called TV quiz payoffs. This sort of newspaper sensationalism can be handled by those who are not in the business, apparently.

But are their skirts as clean as they would like you to believe? What about the Bob Considine story of alleged payola and the same type story of two other well-known columnists? They were buried in the back pages by those who employ them. Payola has been known to exist in the industry for many months. Those who deny they have ever been approached to take payola are perhaps employees of smaller stations in smaller markets or they are record players and not disc jockeys. There is a difference.

What about the buyers in department stores, in grocery stories—"buy one case of my product and you get one free; you buy my blue jeans by the gross or give me your business and I'll remember you at Christmas time." Is this not payola?

Have there not been other accusations of this same sort in the federal government, in the Federal Communications Commission, in the garment industry, in any number of international unions? Payola in one form or another is a part of American business.

This is certainly not to say that I or the broadcasting industry condones the practice, but I say, "Let him who is without sin cast the first stone."[73]

Station officials fired Le Goff for delivering an unauthorized editorial. Would his firing have hit the front page if his dismissal had not been connected with radio? Doubtful. The anchors, in terms of celebrity, were B-list.

It is no wonder that the pattern of local Detroit television news had been set in radio. Many of the early reporters, men such as Clark, Knight, Cederberg, Marshall, and Cline, had worked in radio news, primarily in the Midwest. They had borrowed largely from the older medium as they moved into television. There were bold moves, however. The hiring of Phelps and Dempsey from academia was unusual for the time. In the twenty-first century such a personnel move would be shocking. What stands out is that none of these men were celebrities. They were not written about in the newspapers, except on rare occasions. The "stars" were not in news.

The A-list was reserved for the programming side of television. As radio began as an entertainment medium, so did television. Music shows, comedy, travel, and programs providing household tips were all popular. The stations turned to anybody who could feed this newborn, omnivorous monster. The stations were most interested in anybody who supplied his or her own fresh video material or had a ready appeal for advertisers. Edythe Fern Melrose, who hosted a household tip show, was important to WXYZ-TV because she drew advertising from grocery store chains eager to appeal to young homemakers. Mort Neff, a veteran outdoorsman, had a show that appealed to southeastern Michigan's many hunters and fisherman. In addition, most of the early stars had roots in Detroit.

The stations were particularly interested in sports. The syndicated television programming industry that later provided popular shows such as *The Oprah Winfrey Show* did not exist. NBC was not linked with its midwestern television stations until 1948.[74] The programming void had to be filled locally. Before NBC's Pat Weaver created the *Tonight Show* in the fall of 1954, WWJ-TV filled the 11:30 p.m. time with *The Minnie Jo Show*, a variety show hosted by Minnie Jo Curtis, a local actress. Before the *Today Show* in 1952 and the morning news shows that followed on other networks, Detroit television stations ran religious programming or lectures by college professors. This was the era of *Your Show of Shows* with Sid Caesar and Imogene Coca, which ran between 1950 and 1954, and Milton Berle's *Texaco Star Theater*, the number one show during the 1950–51 television season.[75] Analyst Tim Brooks later called the era "vaudeo—a wedding of vaudeville and the new video medium."[76]

What author John Steinbeck termed "the most powerful means of communication ever devised" was obsessed by sports from the beginning. The appeal was obvious. The audience was ready-made, and the product constantly renewed itself because each football or baseball game was different from the last. WXYZ-TV's opening day broadcasting included broadcasts of three sporting events. WWJ-TV opened with one sporting event, a fencing match, then aired a hockey game on its second day of broadcasting. Even two years later, airing any sort of sporting event, no matter how old, was cause for taking an advertisement out in a newspaper. The University of Michigan Wolverines beat the Minnesota Gophers 27-14 on Saturday, October 23, 1948. WWJ-TV aired the game at 9:00 p.m. the following Tuesday night.[77]

However, the stations could not rely entirely on sports. So they developed their own crop of personalities. WXYZ-TV introduced George Pierrot on October 10, 1948, the station's second day in business. Pierrot, a world traveler, had hosted the Detroit Institute of Arts' World Adventure Series since the 1930s. His presentations involved travel films from around the globe. Pierrot moved the program genre to television and became one of the first stars of the new medium.

Edythe Fern Melrose, "the Lady of Charm," was also highly successful during the 1950s. Her daily program, which aired weekdays on WXYZ-TV between 1948 and 1960, served up a combination of cooking and household tips. Her motto, as relayed to a *Detroit News* reporter in 1945: "A woman's charm depends upon three things—how she acts; how she looks, how she cooks."[78] As she wrote: "Lives of great men all remind us we can make their lives sublime if we learn the art of cooking, and then serve their meals on time."[79] She was compensated well for her work. According to Dick Osgood's *W*Y*X*I*E Wonderland*, a history of WXYZ-TV and WXYZ-AM, Melrose pulled in $100,000 from the two stations in 1952.[80] In 2007 dollars, that is $774,913.[81]

Melrose was especially popular among female viewers. But among youngsters, the first real star to take hold was Soupy Sales. In fifty years of Detroit television, he is Detroit's most recognizable and original star. Baby boomers remember having lunch with Soupy, along with Soupy's TV sidekicks, White Fang and Black Tooth. Boomer parents remember Sales's late-night program. Sales's guest list for the late-night show included jazz artists Charlie Parker, Miles Davis, and Duke Ellington.

At Channel 4, Sonny Eliot emerged and developed into a unique Detroit personality. He was equal parts comedian, weatherman, and Zen master of the new medium. Eliot (real name: Marvin Schlossberg) grew up in Detroit near Hastings and Farnsworth, the son of hardware store owner. Eliot spent hours in the Warfield Theater and became further enamored with show business watching his brother, Leo, work as a big-band drummer.[82]

Fran Stryker, a producer/writer of *The Lone Ranger*, taught Eliot scriptwriting at Wayne State University and helped Eliot get his work on the air. Eliot flew bombing missions during World War II and was shot down in Germany—where he finished the war in a POW camp.[83]

After the war, Eliot began looking around Detroit for opportunities—and decided that television was the place to be. Eliot quickly determined that versatility was his ticket to success. "Whenever somebody asked something, I'd say yes," he said.[84] His other credits included work on a golf show and on *Willy Dooit*, a kids' show. By then, on paper, Eliot would have been perfectly qualified for the job of weatherman. Eliot was one of the few people with actual television experience. As a pilot during World War II, he knew something about weather. The job was his from 1949 to 1981.

Detroit television also paid heed to viewers who loved northern Michigan by introducing *Michigan Outdoors*, which first aired in 1951. Mort Neff's pretelevision career after graduation from the University of Michigan in 1927 included work as a pro tennis player in Monte Carlo and a radio operator on an Arctic expedition. *Michigan Outdoors* ran on WWJ-TV and WXYZ-TV and celebrated Michigan's varied outdoor life. Neff would often head north, but he went south, too. One show featured a trip to Chile in search of trout.

On WJBK-TV, "the Tall Boy in the Third Row," as Bob Murphy was known, drew audiences. He was six feet, eight inches tall. In addition to working as a deejay on WJBK-AM during the 1950s, he was a ubiquitous presence on WJBK-TV, where he hosted *Ladies Day, Breakfast with Murphy*, and *The Morning Show*. Among children's shows, *Milky the Clown* was among the most popular. The show made the phrase "Twin Pines" a part of the Motor City lexicon during the 1950s and 1960s. *Milky's Party Time* debuted on December 16, 1950, becoming a baby boomer favorite during the show's seventeen years on WJBK-TV, WWJ-TV, and WXYZ-TV. Throughout the 1950s, the program was broadcast live from Channel 4's studios in downtown Detroit for two hours on Saturday afternoon. Milky made personal appearances as well. In his white clown outfit, conical hat, white makeup, and dark eye shadow, Milky (as played by magician Clare Cummings) looked slightly surreal. Cummings was a serious magician who won membership in the International Brother of Magicians in 1929. During the week, he worked as a paint salesman for DuPont. The show was great fun: Milky would do his party tricks while parents looked on from a nearby viewing room. The luckiest children would have a chance to dip their hands into a jar of pennies.

That was what Detroit television was during the 1950s and 1960s. It was Mort Neff and the Au Sable River, children dipping their hands in pennies, Soupy Sales getting hit with a pie. With the addition in January 1965 of WKBD-TV, Detroit's first UHF station, the city's television landscape broadened somewhat. The station, located at Channel 50 on the Detroit television dial, programmed mostly sports and movies. It aired no regular newscast until 1978.

In local television, news was considered a loss leader, not a program attraction. This combination of factors, including lack of time and staff, handicapped the journalistic product. The lack of preparation made television reporters particularly susceptible to manipulation. If the news was not taken directly from the network, it was borrowed from local newspapers. One who observed that firsthand from several angles was Jack Casey. Casey had been a *Detroit Free Press* reporter between 1956 and 1962, an executive assistant to Detroit mayor Jerome P. Cavanagh between 1962 and 1966, then a public relations man specializing in politics and public affairs from 1966 until the late 1980s. The lack of knowledge shown by television reporters appalled Casey, who explained:

> They would pick up the *Free Press* in the morning and the *News* in the afternoon and chase those stories. There was almost nothing originated at the TV stations. They were so easy to manipulate, if you wanted to, easy to control. . . . They didn't even try to compete with the papers. They didn't have any journalists, didn't have anybody who really knew what was going on. I'd hate to tell you how many times I'd have so-called reporters from TV come to a news conference or a mayor's meeting, who would say, "What questions should I ask?" They were out there just to splash something on the evening news. It was unabashed, no shame in following the papers because that's all they could do.[85]

Respect from city hall insiders, however, did not matter. Television was becoming lucrative. The medium was a money loser at first, but not for long. The FCC reported that the four television networks on the air, with their ten owned-and-operated stations, along with forty other stations, lost nearly $15 million in 1948.[86] WWJ-TV lost $800,000 during its first two years of operation. The station's dim financial performance was, it seems, irrelevant. "In the face of our losses on WWJ-TV, the owners of the *Detroit News* were calm, game and uncomplaining," wrote Harry Bannister, WWJ-TV's first general manager. "Never once did I hear even a murmur of criticism except 'Let's have more and better programs,' which of course meant more expense and greater losses."[87] Detroit's three stations reported to the FCC they had total revenues of $940,000, 3.4 percent of the total broadcast revenue in the Detroit market. Nationally, radio began showing signs of decline in 1954. Radio revenue dropped in 1954 from the previous year, a first in sixteen years.[88] Detroit radio financial statistics are shown in table 14, and a compilation of Federal Communications statistics on revenue and income of all radio networks and radio stations in the country appears in table 15 (see appendix).

Although data is missing, one can see the outline of the Detroit radio advertising market. Radio station owners in Detroit saw decreases in revenue until the mid-1950s, after which money began to flow again. Some of this may be attributed to an increase in the number of radio stations in the market. Nationally, radio revenue increased each year in the eleven years between 1948 and 1958 except for 1954. But expenses also increased in each year but one. Expenses remained virtually flat between 1954 and 1955. Still, it is clear that radio was no longer the cash machine that it had been immediately after World War II. Profits dropped by roughly one-third by the end of the 1950s.

Compare this with television, which nationally surpassed radio in revenue by 1954, doing so in Detroit by 1953. During that time, television never had a down year, reporting double-digit revenue increases nationally each year. The first decade of television broadcasting saw it run from a business with $8.7 million revenue to a billion-dollar industry. In Detroit the television business went from a $3 million business to a $17 million business in less than a decade. The trajectory was steep, as is illustrated by tables 16 and 17 (see appendix).

One other major change occurred during the 1960s. The change was slow moving but powerful, like a glacier. The major television networks were eating up more and more time of each broadcast day. Consider the figures in table 18 (see appendix). Nobody recognized it at the time, but the network usurpation of television time on local television stations would have implications for news. However, most eyes were focused on the decline of radio and the rise of television. Nationally, the numbers showed that radio had already reached its zenith. Many at first did not see it as it happened. "The big name broadcasters in those years, like H. V. Kaltenborn and Lowell Thomas, avoided television at first," recalled journalist David Brinkley. "It was hard work, there was no money in it, and it was more complicated than radio. H. V. Kaltenborn said to me once, 'I hate television.'"[89] Dr. Frank Stanton, president of CBS, Inc. from 1945 until 1971, reported the reaction of Edward R. Murrow and Eric Sevareid to the early rise of television:

I took Ed to the Century Club one day for lunch and pressed him awful hard to think about doing something in television. This was before he made the switch from "Hear It Now" to "See It Now." Indeed, at the '48 convention in Philadelphia, which was a radio convention although there were cameras down there, we did television. It was miniscule coverage, but at the end of the day we wanted Ed and Eric to come into the studio and talk a little bit about what had happened. Ed didn't want to do it on television; he wanted to do it on radio.[90]

The world of television would move on, despite Murrow's wishes. Four years after Murrow debated Stanton, a new CBS employee by the name of Walter Cronkite became a star, a result of his television work during the 1952 political conventions. As illustrated by the financial tables discussed above, the money flowed into the new medium. Network radio was finished, going from an important source of information in 1945 to a sideshow only fifteen years later. But television, like radio in the 1920s and much of the 1930s, still had a "silly" quality about it. Radio had been Murrow and Kaltenborn and Swing. Television was Milton Berle and the crooked quiz shows and Lucille Ball. The day of the omniscient news analysts who could hold forth intelligently on any number of serious topics was finished. In radio, news analysts such as Kaltenborn, Swing, Elmer Davis, and others made money for the medium. In television, this was not the case. As analyst Quincy Howe wrote: "The news analyst . . . faces two handicaps [in television]. First, if he is worth his salt and goes in for controversy most local sponsors and stations will have none of him. Second, the news analyst who is worth his salt will not voice his own commercials. Few postwar commentators, I must add, have had to grapple with the temptation to read their own commercials, for the simple reason that few sponsors wanted them on any terms." Besides, as Howe pointed out, television was a new medium. NBC programming chief Pat Weaver had introduced the concept of the "spectacular" during the early 1950s in which a line of experts was brought in to talk about certain topics. Howe, an analyst himself, believed that Weaver's idea had finished off the old-fashioned radio analyst. "On the one hand, Weaver's innovations promised to liberate some news analysts from the necessity of having to fill the same time period at the same hour of every day, no matter how much or little there might be to talk about at that moment," wrote Howe. "On the other hand, these same innovations threatened to liberate other news analysts from their jobs by opening the door to assorted experts to cover special situations as they arose."[91]

Curiously, newspapermen seemed to understand the challenges of the new medium as well as anybody. Newspaper owners, after a period of resistance, had decided the radio and newspapers could coexist. So, too, they had apparently decided that television and newspaper could coexist. The attitudes can best be expressed by examining meetings of the American Society of Newspaper Editors (ASNE). These meetings, an annual gathering of the people who ran the country's newspapers, would be akin to a convention of cardinals. They were the deans of journalism, and they were all there in 1950 and 1951, editors of newspapers big and small: John S. Knight, chief of the burgeoning Knight Newspapers empire; Lester Markel, Sunday editor of the *New York Times;* Whitelaw Reid, editor of the *New York Herald-Tribune;* and Hodding Carter, editor of the *Delta (MS) Democrat-Times.* They met in the spring of 1951 in Washington, DC's Hotel Statler. One item on the April 20, 1951, agenda was "The Challenge of Radio and Television to Newspapers." The discussion clearly indicated this group's thoughts about the electronic media that confronted their journalistic preeminence, ranging from hostility to ambivalence. Radio had grown as a serious news medium during World War II. And television, barely three years from the cradle and reaching more people every day, looked as if it was about to enter the game. Their world was about to change. They knew that.

The man who spoke against the influence of radio and television was E. C. Hoyt, managing editor of the *Cedar Rapids (IA) Gazette.* Hoyt knew he was speaking to a crowd that had already accepted television. "I have already become a typed character, a sort of hound of the airwaves, and when there was no one else to take this role of opening up the criticism of radio and television, they called on me," he told the delegates. He warned the crowd that they "might wake up some day and find the props washed out from under them." Hoyt had a lot to say on the matter. "Radio merely skims the cream of news. . . . Television newsmen look for the dramatic, something to make a good show. But first thing you know TV will be making the people think it is providing all the news they need."[92]

But none of the panel members agreed with him. Ralph E. McGill, editor of the *Atlanta Constitution,* argued, "[W]hile there definitely is a challenge to newspapers, neither radio nor television necessarily will destroy us."[93] It would seem that newspaper executives, right from the start, saw television as a supplement to journalism, not as direct competition.

And when the editors met the next year, again at the Statler, they revisited the topic. Ralph D. Casey, director of the University of Minnesota's school of journalism, brought a survey that showed McGill had been correct the year before, at least as far as Minnesota readers were concerned. "Our research does not support the alarming forecasts that have been made about the effects of TV on newspaper reading," Casey told the crowd. Wallace Lomoe, managing editor of the *Milwaukee Journal*, agreed. Lomoe saw "not so much a problem as an opportunity." He talked about television as "a highlighter, or reminder, putting a focus on news."[94]

As it turned out, Casey may have been right. Perhaps television was skimming the news. Perhaps television was too eager for a show. But McGill and Lomoe had been more right than Casey. Although television grew into a mass medium within ten years, the money flowed in the direction of newspapers, as it always had. Perhaps the stream did not flow with such magnitude as it had in the past, but not all newspapers were damaged.

However, afternoon newspapers began bleeding heavily after the appearance of television news. In Detroit, Hearst's *Detroit Times* lost circulation during the 1950s, eventually closing in 1960 (see appendix, table 19). It would be difficult to establish a direct cause-and-effect relationship between the rise of television and the death of the *Detroit Times*. But as the chart shows, the newspaper lost 7.5 percent of its weekday circulation and 21.3 percent of its Sunday circulation before the Evening News Association purchased it in November 1960 and shuttered the publication. Evening newspapers, including the *Detroit News*, would face difficulty surviving in a world in which people could watch the day's news at 6:00 p.m. instead of reading yesterday's news at 5:00 p.m.

The fifteen-minute newscasts provided by the television networks and local stations were little more than headline services with pictures. But television was becoming lucrative enough that the medium could afford to begin building a journalism presence. Detroit local television had shown what it could do with a big news story when it aired two days of U.S. Senate Crime Committee hearings. Soon, television news would begin getting the airtime to develop into something more than a headline service.

3. TELEVISION NEWS DEVELOPS

Television news would become more than a headline service during the 1960s. Before then, television news had little on-air time, which was (and is) the most vital real estate in broadcasting. That changed during the decade. Time devoted to news in Detroit and at the three television networks expanded, but for different reasons. WXYZ-TV committed itself to local news after a chain of events that began with a meeting between ABC's chairman and a powerful U.S. senator. Advertising sales considerations caused Detroit's stations to expand from fifteen-minute newscasts to thirty minutes. WWJ-TV ruled the world of Detroit television journalism. But WXYZ-TV and WJBK-TV became ambitious new players in broadcast journalism—each using a different approach.

A new generation of television news evolved on September 2, 1963, with the debut of network television's first thirty-minute evening newscast. Until that evening in 1963, network television newscasts, and most local television newscasts, routinely ran fifteen minutes. As CBS News producer Ernest Leiser wrote in a memo to top CBS corporate management, the fifteen-minute format allowed only for a "compressed, tabloid treatment" of the day's news. The new format, argued Leiser, would allow for "more news of more kinds, and we will give that news new meaning."[1] CBS News president Richard S. Salant, looking back at the innovation, argued, "It is clear that the half-hour news had significance vastly beyond the addition of fifteen minutes. Network evening news became not just twice as long and twice as important; it was a quantum jump. . . . quarter of an hour may not seem like much in a person's lifetime, but for network television news, it was a revolution."[2]

The revolution occurred after two years of difficult debate, both internally at CBS and with network affiliates. Salant wrote that some network executives worried whether "viewers would sit still for a whole half hour." They were also anxious about whether CBS News could fill thirty minutes nightly. But the toughest debate was with CBS affiliates. They had the power to derail the project despite the network's best intentions. As Salant later related: "[N]ot surprisingly, affiliates did not want to yield the time they were occupying to the network."[3] Every minute of airtime taken by the network was one minute less that could be filled by the affiliate. More important, it was less potential advertising time that could be peddled by the local station. With fifteen minutes of local news and fifteen minutes of network news, local stations had a neat, half-hour package. Finally, CBS issued an ultimatum. It would proceed with thirty minutes of news—take it or leave it. "Station after station threatened to leave it," wrote Walter Cronkite, "but, failing to bluff CBS, by the time the big day came they fell into line almost without exception."[4]

NBC News' *Huntley-Brinkley Report* followed with a thirty-minute newscast one week later. ABC did not follow with thirty minutes of nightly news until 1967, forty months after its two competitors. The debut of both CBS's and NBC's longer broadcasts featured interviews with President John F. Kennedy. Perhaps as important was the competition that had developed between the two news organizations. The contest was fought not by adding frothy entertainment elements to draw viewers, but with serious journalism.

Two examples stand out, both occurring during the first week of September 1963. In an effort to counter publicity surrounding the CBS News expansion, NBC News ran a three-hour prime-time examination of the civil rights battles in the South. Although not directly competing during the early evening with the Cronkite broadcast, NBC television replaced its entire prime-time schedule with a night of serious journalism. "The NBC special, 'The American Revolution of 1963,' must stand as a turning point in TV's journalistic evolution," wrote *New York Times* critic Jack Gould. "Never before has so much valuable prime time been accorded to a single domestic social issue in one uninterrupted stretch."[5] And on the day that NBC's Chet Huntley and David Brinkley inaugurated their thirty-minute newscast, CBS ran an interview with Republican Barry Goldwater, who had previously vowed not to speak with CBS News because of the network's coverage of the conservative movement.

Documentaries and aggressive reporting were not new in television. Edward R. Murrow produced historic documentaries during the 1950s on U.S. senator Joseph McCarthy (R-WI), the plight of migrant workers in Florida, and smoking, all in the context of his acclaimed *See It Now* program. But the thirty-minute newscast started a new epoch in television news at the network-television level, eventually spreading to Detroit and other local stations. An examination of random samples of television schedules shows serious documentaries much in evidence during the early and mid-1960s, both nationally and locally. On September 19, 1963, NBC News ran a one-hour documentary, "Experiment to Excellence," about trends on education. In addition, WWJ-TV televised a one-hour town meeting, live from the station's auditorium, in which Michigan governor George Romney took questions. On June 18, 1964, ABC News aired a 30-minute special about Democratic vice presidential possibilities; on the same evening, NBC News anchor David Brinkley visited Salem, New Jersey, and explored the town's political attitudes.

What was even more significant was the team Salant chose to carry out the task at CBS. Journalistic considerations were important, show business considerations seemingly few. Douglas Edwards, who had anchored the news throughout the 1950s, was an adequate journalist. But he was mostly a "reader." His successor at the anchor desk, Walter Cronkite, was a far more experienced newsman. He had been a key United Press correspondent during World War II, working under Harrison Salisbury, who was to become one of the most important journalists of his generation. Cronkite, who strongly favored print experience for broadcasters, thought "it's absolutely fundamental that young journalists serve an apprenticeship or something more than that on newspapers and on a wire service, too, before they try television. . . . A young man starting in television never has the opportunity to learn how to get a story, to organize it and to develop a respect for facts as he would if a tough, competitive city editor drilled these things into him."[6] Salant describes Cronkite as "tough, passionately insistent on objectivity and fairness. Above all, he was always checking to make sure the facts were right. He was, in short, both a great reporter and a great editor." Eric Sevareid was chosen as an analyst for the nightly newscast. Salant described Sevareid as "an artist among craftsman. . . . Some people write beautifully; some people think clearly and brilliantly. Few can do both. Eric was one of the few."[7] It should be noted, however, that both men also came off well on television. Cronkite had a baritone voice and a credible appearance, while the square-jawed Sevareid could have played the cinema version of an ambassador or U.S. senator. Still, there were many possible anchors who looked and sounded as good or better than Sevareid and Cronkite. But Sevareid and Cronkite got the job.

Salant had what might be described as an antitelevision, anti–show business bias. As Salant related in his memoirs: "In television, we tend to be bemused by the business of pictures. But over and over again, at every opportunity, I reminded my colleagues that in journalism, words are of prime importance. I came to believe that too often pictures did not add to a story but subtracted from it."[8]

Much of CBS's new aggressiveness was in response to the success of NBC News. Since pairing anchors Chet Huntley and David Brinkley at the 1956 Democratic and Republican conventions, the news division had had an unqualified string of successes. NBC president Robert Kintner, a former reporter, pushed NBC News to a new loftiness. "Kintner emphasized news programs as never before, or since, on any network," wrote Reuven Frank, who later became NBC News president. "There was money for reporters; there was money for documentaries; there was money for special programs. . . . The great weight of his presence was for more news, and news more prominently displayed."[9] Chet Huntley, for instance, hosted his own news program, *Chet Huntley Reporting*, which aired between 1957 and 1963.[10] It was Kintner who talked Gulf Oil into bankrolling a series of "instant specials." Major news would break, NBC News would commandeer airtime, and Gulf Oil would pay the bill.

Local television news was growing, too. Most dramatic, perhaps, was KNXT-TV, the CBS-owned station in Los Angeles, which expanded its early evening news offering to ninety minutes at 6:00 p.m. weekdays in September 1963.[11]

But something else was going on in Detroit that would eventually change the course of television news across the country: Storer Broadcasting began employing the services of a research consultant, McHugh and Hoffman, Inc. The firm would eventually become the biggest and most influential company in the field, divining attitudes for more than a hundred television stations in markets big and small across the United States, and creating the "Eyewitness News" format—a new genre of local news broadcasting that would change journalism. Founder Philip McHugh had previously run the television division of the Campbell-Ewald Company, a Detroit-based advertising agency that handled the Chevrolet account. His division also produced network variety programs, including *The Dinah Shore Show*, *The Chevy Show* (with Dinah Shore and Bob Hope), and *Chevrolet on Broadway*.[12] McHugh left Campbell-Ewald in 1962, taking associate

Peter S. Hoffman with him. The two opened a small office at 470 North Woodward in Birmingham.

They worked closely with W. Lloyd Warner, a sociologist who founded Chicago-based Social Research Inc. Warner spent much of his professional life studying this country's class system. "Because a given individual occupies a particular place in the social space of a given society, out of a multitude of places it would be possible for him to be in, and participates in this one place," Warner wrote in his classic *The Social Life of a Modern Community*, "he has a social personality different from that of anyone else."[13] Where a person worshipped, a person's job, what kinds of magazines and newspapers (if any) a person read, where a person lived, the type of music a person enjoyed, all placed that person firmly somewhere in an informal caste system.

Television ratings would tell a broadcast executive, in rough terms, how many viewers were watching a particular program. But they had little information on demographics, other than age. Warner developed a sophisticated class model of urban society in which income and education were only two of the variables used for analysis. Social Research Inc.'s research reports hinged on the concept of social class:

> Social class refers to the large grouping of people who share common values and styles of life, and who are seen both by themselves and others as occupying a particular status relative to the rest of the community, high, medium, or low. Social classes are not income groups, per se. Each social class contains a considerable range in income. Young families in the upper middle and upper classes frequently have lower incomes than middle-aged families in the upper lower class. More importantly, the concept of social class grew out of recognition that income and community status are often disparate.[14]

McHugh and Hoffman researchers, using Warner's model, broke urban America and metro Detroit into five groups:

1. The upper class, the smallest of the five groups, measuring perhaps 2 percent of metro Detroit's population: It was "made up of the inheritors of high status, plus newly-rich or newly-accomplished families with polish, ambition, and/or personal charm, who have gained social

acceptance into the leadership ranks of their respective communities." Because of the group's small numbers, McHugh and Hoffman argued it could safely be ignored.

2. The upper-middle class, which made up 11 percent of the metro Detroit television viewership: these were "primarily the managerial and professional people of the urban scene; as a rule, they are considerably above average in education, sophistication, cultural interests, and public spiritedness."

3. The lower-middle class—which was 28 percent of metro Detroit's population, according to McHugh and Hoffman estimates. A report called this group "the 'ciphers' of the nation's business class—plus the top level of skilled blue-collar workers. These people are very concerned about their social standing in the eyes of their fellow citizens; they live on the 'right side of the tracks,' they 'keep up with the Joneses.'" The group's taste was characterized as "all-American middle-brow."

4. The upper-lower class—the largest segment of the metro Detroit population at 42 percent. This demographic included tens of thousands of Detroit's blue-collar assembly line workers. "These people mostly live relatively quiet lives of 'getting by' and enjoying what they can afford from day to day. They are not so concerned with 'what other people think,' but they are very eager to be 'up with the times,' take advantage of modern conveniences, and share in the Good Life, U.S.A."

5. The lower-lower class—17 percent of metro Detroit. These were the "down-and-outers, its social and financial outcasts. In most urban centers it is dominantly composed of ex-hillbillies, Puerto Ricans, Mexicans, and the poorer half of Negroes."[15]

What is striking is that the concept of research had not been applied to local television newsrooms. The business world attached importance to the measurement of public attitudes, particularly in industries that depended on anticipating shifting public tastes. But the idea of gauging market attitudes about a television station and its news personalities had never been attempted.

McHugh and Hoffman counseled clients to program for the masses. A programmer who aimed for "Joe Six-Pack"—the lower-middle class and the upper-lower class—would be shooting at the big target: 70 percent of the population.

The company's first research report for WJBK-TV, delivered in July of 1962, illustrated WWJ-TV's dominance in the market. Through its association with Social Research, Inc., the company interviewed 436 metro Detroit respondents. It found that WWJ-TV was "clearly the "prestige station in Detroit," not to mention the preferred station among viewers (see appendix, table 20). The sources of the station's popularity were many, according to McHugh. WWJ-TV's association with NBC helped. Its link with the *Detroit News* was an even bigger help. The researchers wrote:

> A major ingredient of WWJ's strength in Detroit is the association between it and the Detroit News. Approximately 59% of the men and women in our sample who were asked about station ownership volunteered the information that "the News owns WWJ." For this 59%, this fact about WWJ is important in their deciding that it is "a high type station—I always think of it as quality" and recognizing that "it is one of the oldest and best local stations." The News is an old, powerful, and successful institution on the Detroit scene, and there is a minimum of animosity directed toward it. By and large, it is a well-liked paper, and these attitudes of respect and approval of the News carry over in modified forms to WWJ in people's feelings about it.[16]

McHugh's initial research detailed other elements behind WWJ-TV's power in the market. Anchorman Dick Westerkamp was viewed as something of an "everyman." According to the research, "He probably has never created a controversy in his adult life. He is fine and upstanding. He is not particularly engaging or charming; he does not try to win the audience through gimmicks; in, he is not quite a 'personality.' He is most clearly only an 'announcer' who is taking both the responsibilities of his job and the news itself quite clearly."[17]

Detroiters also liked weatherman Sonny Eliot. "The Channel 4 performer who does most to put humor and enjoyability into the picture is weatherman Sunny [*sic*] Eliot. These is no other personality on the Detroit television scene who is talked about so much and so freely, pro and con, as Eliot. Most of the talk is 'pro' and revolves around the zany antics and comments he inserts into his weathercasting," McHugh wrote.[18]

But two other personalities on the WWJ-TV schedule particularly appealed to Detroiters, according to the research: George Pierrot and Mort Neff.

> Locality and friendliness of a different sort [from Sonny Eliot] are brought into WWJ by George Pierrot and Morton Neff. As these men are described by the respondents in our sample, they are essentially pleasant individuals who communicate considerable expertise and enthusiasm for travel, outdoor life, and the state of Michigan. All of these facts—pleasantness, expertness, enthusiasms and love of Michigan—contribute to their appeal as television personalities and to the appeal of their programs. The last mentioned facet above is particularly important, because Michigan and Detroiters are uncommonly fascinated by, and "in love" with, their state.[19]

Most important, though was McHugh's description of what viewers wanted from a newscast. There was no talk of democracy in action, an informed public, the importance of words, or anything else one might hear from CBS's Richard Salant or from a university journalism professor. Since the advent of McHugh and Hoffman's success and the creation of the news consultancy business, there had been much discussion about the role of consultants in newsrooms. Later, some would denounce them as a force behind the "dumbing down" of television. Here is what McHugh told WJBK-TV officials about viewer preferences when it came to news. It is worth quoting at length, because this became the reigning philosophy of the local television news industry:

> What people want to hear is whether anything has happened, nationally, internationally, statewide, or locally, which they ought to know about or is something which may possibly affect their own lives or those of their friends, neighbors, acquaintances, etc. At this hour a certain amount of impatience develops whenever a newscaster starts out by dwelling on a lot of abstract issues and controversies, or on distant and unexciting events which do not directly affect the lives of Detroiters or of people like one's own self, or are not the material of tomorrow's conversation. . . . What people want, in other words, is the nearest thing to a complete inventory of any and every thing interesting which has

gone on since they last read a newspaper or heard a broadcast of news. Whenever an announcer seems to be dawdling, a worry develops in the viewer's mind that the announcer is not going to have time to mention everything that could or should be brought up. . . . This is not to say that people want a hurried and exciting tracking down of the news; rather, they would like a calm and assuring recital of what has gone on (which for all its calmness and assurance still moves along at a brisk pace.)[20]

With that in mind, McHugh recommended the development of a strong news personality at the station.

The research company continued with annual reports. Within two years, McHugh and Hoffman began to notice weaknesses in WWJ-TV's seemingly unassailable armor. "WWJ-TV remains the 'home station' in Detroit, but its image is beginning to wear a little thin," McHugh and Hoffman wrote in a report two years later. "It is still the favored station for news and doing the most for the city, but it is now beginning to be seen as somewhat stuffy and less entertaining, principally due to NBC programming, but partially due to the expansion of the early evening 90 minutes of information programming. Its primary appeal is in the upper classes and older people." The report also stated: "Public service programming continues to have a low level of appeal to Detroit viewers. The very small element that favors these programs are those crusading for some cause or those with problems they feel need solving, such as the Negroes. Upper-middle class viewers are tolerant of public service programming for the effect they feel it has on informing the classes below them. But, for themselves, they prefer the printed media for keeping informed."[21] The ratings showed WWJ-TV's strength as late as 1965 (see appendix, table 21).

Working with the McHugh and Hoffman recommendations, WJBK-TV put together a news operation that would later be described as "the New York Yankees" of local television news.[22] The recommendation that the station develop a strong news personality was accomplished almost by default. Jac Le Goff developed into this "news personality." Many Detroiters had heard about Le Goff's firing at WJBK-TV. But that did not necessarily hurt the newscaster's image. Wrote McHugh: "All he [Le Goff] has is the record of a controversial figure, but he seems to have neither the flair nor color of a controversialist. . . . The vast majority of Detroiters never seem to have really known what the argument was all about, except that it was between the station and Le Goff and did not involve any issue or principle the public cared much about."[23]

By 1964 Le Goff had turned into the station's top news personality—the person McHugh had recommended the station hire. "Without hurting the team spirit that is developing, a definite 'head man' should be evident to viewers," wrote McHugh in his next report. He continued: "Because of his increased popularity, this role naturally falls to Jac Le Goff."[24] In the margin of McHugh's files, the word "done" is scribbled in the margin.

The researchers had further thoughts about what drew Detroit television viewers to the newscast. Those thoughts were underlined, in case WJBK-TV officials might fail to notice them:

1. *They want the news presented in a palatable way, easy to comprehend and with the harshness of everyday events "softened" for them.*
2. *They want a newscast that is trustworthy. One that is delivered in a relaxed manner that gives them a complete and unbiased report of events.*
3. *They want a newscast to make them feel more a part of the community.*[25]

By the mid-1960s, each of Detroit's television stations also had thirty-minute newscasts. WXYZ-TV was the first to make the move, going to a thirty-minute news broadcast during the late afternoon. WJBK-TV and WWJ-TV each expanded by 1966. However, there was a certain sleight of hand involved in the change. Before the mid-1960s, as previously noted, news, weather, and sports programs each stood alone. News might air for fifteen minutes, weather for five minutes, and sports for five minutes. Each had its own sponsor. For instance, National Bank of Detroit sponsored WWJ-TV's newscast for a time. So did Richman Brothers clothiers. Each program had its own rhythm, its own beginning, middle, and end. In the new thirty-minute format, news, sports, and weather were collapsed into one program. Detroit viewers were not, in fact, seeing twice as much news as before, as they were on the Cronkite and Huntley-Brinkley broadcasts. Sports and weather were not added to the CBS and NBC nightly newscasts, although other "back of the book" elements (as coverage of cultural stories and features stories had been dubbed) were now included. In Detroit, however, viewers were seeing virtually the same amount of local news as before. But now, the news anchor, sportscaster, and weathercaster shared the same set. As this study will demonstrate later, this opened the door for more show business possibilities.

James F. Clark explained that the old format was a holdover from radio:

> When these things first started out, people would buy programs. And then it evolved from buying programs to buying spots in programs. It was easier to sell spots in a half-hour show than it was [in a show of] fifteen minutes, then a break, then five, then a break. . . . It evolved into a thing where, well, they weren't going to buy programs; they were going to buy spots in programs. So the management decided to repackage the whole thing and make it a half hour of news. So we started promoting a half hour of news. It didn't change the content any. It just changed the way they were packaging it.[26]

That was not the only trend. Local stations began surrendering more time to their networks in the 1960s. That number would grow from 57 percent in 1963 to 66 percent thirty years later. Even more important, the syndicated television programming industry began to boom in the 1960s. Syndicated programs such as those hosted by Mike Douglas and Merv Griffin jumped from 2 percent of a station's weekly program time to 9 percent, a fivefold swell.[27]

Each of Detroit's three stations more than doubled the amount of time devoted to news during the sixties (see appendix, tables 22–24). WJBK-TV's news time went from forty-five minutes each day at the start of the decade to two hours at the end. The station's fifteen-minute broadcasts at 6:00 p.m. and 11:00 p.m. each expanded to thirty minutes. Similarly, WWJ-TV's news offering went from forty minutes daily in 1960 to two hours and five minutes by decade's end. There, too, the 6:00 p.m. and 11:00 p.m. newscasts had expanded to thirty minutes by 1966. WXYZ-TV finally entered the news business in a serious way. The station had aired as little as five minutes of news in the late 1950s. By 1968 it had become a contender, airing ninety minutes daily. This included Detroit's first sixty-minute early evening news broadcast.

The one-hour newscast was emblematic of WXYZ-TV's new embrace of television news. The new interest started at the very top of ABC, working its way to its five owned-and-operated stations. Although ABC News did not become truly competitive with CBS News and NBC News until the late 1970s and early 1980s, the American Broadcasting Company began taking news seriously in the early 1960s, after ABC chairman Leonard Goldenson had been summoned to Washington, DC, by one of the most powerful men in Congress. Goldenson recalled:

Just after Kennedy was elected President, in November 1960, I had a call from Senator John Pastore. He chaired the Senate Communications Subcommittee, which had oversight of the broadcasting industry.

Pastore asked me down to Washington. "I know you're making progress and I know you've been losing money, but I think you've got to start addressing yourself to the news problem," he said. "If you're ever going to build ABC in the eyes of the Senate and the House—in Washington, generally—you're going to have to build your own news operation.[28]

The network developed a series, *Focus on America*, which aired during the summers of 1961, 1962, and 1963 and featured the best documentaries originating from ABC stations across the country.[29] WXYZ-TV contributed two such documentaries. The new series may have been aired during the summer, when viewership is light, but it was a serious effort. WXYZ-TV contributed an examination of the emergency room of Detroit Receiving Hospital, and "Within My Walls," which featured the Detroit Institute of Arts.[30] The ABC News division also produced *ABC News Reports* in 1963–64, which included a five-part series entitled "Crucial Summer: The 1963 Civil Rights Crisis." Former CBS newsman Howard K. Smith was hired in 1962 to anchor "Howard K. Smith—News and Comment," which aired in 1962 and 1963.[31]

ABC's resurgence had come after James C. Hagerty, President Dwight D. Eisenhower's former press secretary, had taken over as vice president of news, special events, and public affairs. Hagerty had extensive experience both in and out of government, first as a *New York Times* reporter (1934–43) and later as an executive assistant to Governor Thomas E. Dewey. Hagerty had worked with General Eisenhower during Eisenhower's 1952 presidential campaign, and served as his presidential press secretary throughout his two terms.[32] After joining ABC News, he managed to lure some of his generation's best newsmen to ABC. Bill Lawrence of the *New York Times* had received offers from both CBS News and NBC News at various times during his career, but chose to come to work for Hagerty after a tiff with *Times* management. Howard K. Smith joined ABC News after a philosophical dispute with CBS chairman William S. Paley. Hagerty wanted to build a news division, and that meant building news at the ABC-owned stations in New York, Los Angeles, Chicago, San Francisco, and Detroit. According to WXYZ-TV program director Peter Strand, "When Jim Haggerty joined ABC as their news head, he was interested in having owned-and-operated stations get into news. That's how we got into news—not only us, but also WBKB in Chicago and KGO in San Francisco. So we all got into the news business, almost overnight. It was our job to develop a local news operation. So we did."[33]

WXYZ-TV general manager John Pival had been ordered by his corporate superiors at ABC headquarters to develop a news department. "I don't believe for a minute that he sat around at the grill of the Oakland Hills Country Club thinking, 'I've got to get into news,'" said Dave Diles, a sportscaster hired by Pival. "He always thought he could make more money with Soupy Sales getting a pie in the face. But once he got into it, he got into it with both feet."[34]

There were other reasons for local and national expansion, notably a series of unprecedented national crises. The years between 1963 and 1968 saw the assassination of the president of the United States and two of the country's top political leaders, the escalation of a war in Southeast Asia, scores of urban riots, and the transformation of the civil rights struggle into the black power movement. Locally, there was much to report about. That included an exciting young mayor of the city of Detroit, Jerome P. Cavanagh; two important national labor leaders, Teamster president James Hoffa and Walter P. Reuther, president of the United Auto Workers union; the rewriting of the Michigan Constitution; and the rise of George Romney, who within a half dozen years of his 1962 election as governor of Michigan would become a major Republican presidential candidate. In addition, the "Big Three," General Motors Corporation, Ford Motor Company, and Chrysler Corporation, were at the crest of their industrial power and influence. Add to this one of the largest African American populations north of the Mason-Dixon line and you had a turbulent era with much to talk about.

However, WXYZ-TV's method in choosing an anchorman contrasted sharply with the way CBS News' Richard Salant had chosen Walter

Cronkite only a year or two earlier. Salant had been impressed with Cronkite's newsgathering skills. Leon McNew, who was chosen to anchor WXYZ-TV's new newscast, had no journalism experience before moving to the news department as its most visible representative. He had been an announcer on the *Lady of Charm* program, had hosted movies as "Captain Flint," and even did a parody of Mike Wallace on Soupy Sales's late-night entertainment program, playing the character Mike Walters. According to Dick Osgood, a WXYZ-TV on-air talent who later wrote a history of the station, this is the way McNew's audition went:

> McNew was handed some copy and read it. His face wore a natural expression of relaxed vigor, his white hair gave an impression of authority, and he was not pompous.
>
> "Well—he looks good," [Channel 7 news director Richard] Femmel conceded.
>
> [WXYZ-TV general manager John] Pival picked up the phone and dialed control.
>
> "Tell Lee he's our news man."[35]

By 1962 the station was in the news business at 11:00 p.m. Instead of running entertainment programs at that hour, it aired a fifteen-minute national news broadcast from ABC News and the fifteen-minute *Big News* program with anchors McNew and sportscaster Dave Diles.[36]

Unlike McNew, Diles was a product of print and wire service journalism. Before joining WXYZ-TV in 1961, he never drew a paycheck from a television station. His background included work at Associated Press and on small newspapers in Ohio. Diles's entry into television was literally a matter of being at the right place at the right time. He had finished emceeing an event at the Redford Western Golf and Country Club one evening when a man in sunglasses approached him. "I'd like to hire you," said the man. Replied Diles: "Why don't you call me in the event that you sober up?" The man in the sunglasses was John Pival. "Television was an accident," Diles explained.[37]

The man Pival chose to run the WXYZ-TV newsroom was more like Diles and less like McNew, deeply committed to traditional journalistic values. The new leader was news director William Fyffe, a graduate of Northwestern University's Medill School of Journalism and a veteran reporter from WWJ-TV. Colleagues described Fyffe as an "old-fashioned newsman." Jim Herrington, a college classmate of Fyffe, knew that "when Fyffe got to Channel 7, things would change." Continued Herrington: "Fyffe was a kind of an old-fashioned, hard-nosed news guy, except he realized that television was here to stay. He had no problem with innovations, doing things that nobody had done before. But still, Fyffe was an old-fashioned newsman. You just did it right, did it honestly. You followed it up, and checked and checked and checked. The fact that we used cameras and smoke and mirrors made no difference. The old rules still applied as far as Fyffe was concerned."[38]

WXYZ-TV officials raided the local radio stations for news talent, notably WKNR-AM. All of the new hires had at least some journalism experience. Although WKNR-AM was a teen rock station, owner Nellie Knorr believed in building a news operation to give the station credibility with advertisers. The station ran news at fifteen minutes and forty-five minutes after the hour, twenty-four hours a day, seven days a week. Many of the most important figures in Detroit television journalism, including Bill Bonds, had worked at the station. The news chief was Phil Nye, who later went on to two tours as WXYZ-TV news director, and as a vice president for news for the ABC-owned stations. Nye and the department produced long-playing records each year between 1964 and 1968 recapping and analyzing news in metropolitan Detroit.

Two of three reporters hired by Fyffe were native Detroiters with lengthy experience in radio news. The third was a former classmate of Fyffe from Northwestern University. The first reporter hired was Barney Morris. A graduate of the University of Detroit, Morris worked radio in the 1950s and became news director at WCAR-AM during the early 1960s. One of his employees was Bill Bonds. Morris soon learned about the mercurial nature of radio. "The station owner came in one day and wanted me to fire pretty much the entire news department. I thought everybody was doing a good job, including Bill, and wouldn't do it. So the owner fired me."[39] He ended up at WJBK-AM as a newsman, and eventually went across the hall to WJBK-TV as a part-time sportscaster subbing for Bill Flemming.

The next hire in 1964 was WKNR-AM newsman Bill Bonds, who turned into the first local on-air television news personality to realize the medium's dramatic possibilities. Before Bonds, people like Dick Westerkamp,

Carl Cederberg, and Jac Le Goff were the norm. They were solid, credible, informed and unexcitable, unemotional. These are all fine qualities for a newsman. But Bonds felt that the television medium's potential for dramatic communication was untapped. As he related in an interview: "You would have these guys—Westerkamp and Le Goff—practically ignoring what they were reading. If a busload of nuns were killed and raped on Belle Isle, they would have no reaction. [Speaking in a flat monotone]: 'A busload of Roman Catholic nuns were raped and killed on Belle Isle today. Police suspect foul play.' This was no way to do the news. You had to grab 'em by the lapels."[40]

Bonds grew up on Twelfth Street near Burlingame. He was congenitally argumentative and intellectually curious—qualities not much appreciated in his youth. He was kicked out of one Catholic school after another and earned lukewarm grades. He joined the U.S. Army, graduated from the University of Detroit, and worked at a string of radio stations, usually just at the edge of breaking through. WJR-AM executives took a look at him, but passed. Bonds auditioned for WWJ-TV news director James Clark, but Bonds's ego bothered Clark. "The newsroom was known as the 'ego's nest,'" Clark reported. "The last thing we needed was another big ego in there."[41] Sonny Eliot arranged for an interview with other TV executives, but Bonds did not show.

Serendipity helped break him out of the radio business and into television. Bonds had been working as a city hall reporter for WKNR-AM. He was tenacious. Covering a tornado in Anchor Bay and unable to transmit his story, he climbed a telephone pole, used alligator clips to establish a connection to his newsroom, and reported his stories. His first newscast of the day was 4:45 a.m. He would do the morning news, then head out to cover Detroit Common Council and city hall. Mayor Jerome P. Cavanagh liked Bonds, even offering him a job as a speechwriter. ("I didn't take it," Bonds later explained, "because my ego would have gotten in the way. I thought I should be the guy making policy.")[42]

With this trio in harness, the station started a color newscast, a big move in those days, and needed credible, productive reporters to fill the time and mold themselves into a team. The other reporter snared by WXYZ-TV was Jim Herrington, who had been hired from Flint. Bonds remembered the change in attitude at the station:

At some point, I think it was in the mid-1960s, the research started to show that the station that was number one in news was number one in a lot of other things. So there was a big push from on top, mainly from Dick O'Leary, president of the ABC owned-and-operated stations. So you had O'Leary. And you had Leonard Goldenson [chairman of ABC], who had a soft spot in his heart for Channel 7. Goldenson built the station, and would come by every year to speak to the employees. At a certain point, we could get anything we wanted. If we needed new cameras, new editing equipment, whatever it was, we got it. The attitude was "Tell us what you need to do your job and we'll give it to you."[43]

At first, the ratings were miserable: "Everybody beat us," Herrington reported. "One time, the ratings book came up and showed we were being beaten by Huckleberry Finn [the cartoon character, shown on WKBD-TV], but that was OK. We knew we were getting better." WXYZ-TV, led by Fyffe, shared a fascination with using the new medium to its fullest potential. "You would hear from other people in television about 'speaking to the millions,'" said Herrington. "But I thought that was all wrong. We were in the business of communicating one-on-one with our viewers. That's what I tried to do. And that's what Bill Bonds did."[44]

Bad ratings or not, Detroit television had a new competitor, and a hungry one at that. The new competitor had ideas about the television medium, ones that took into account the medium's dramatic potential. This would become extremely important by July 23, 1967.

Money, it would seem, was available to everybody (see appendix, tables 25–26). Detroit television revenue was extremely robust, with stations reporting double-digit percentage revenue increases in five of ten years, and double-digit percentage profit increases in four of ten. What's more, Detroit's newspaper industry labor problems were a boon to the Detroit television stations. Television and radio industry revenue grew 20 percent and 23 percent respectively in 1964, when a 134-day strike closed both newspapers. The revenue flowed even more in 1967, when another strike closed both newspapers for nine months in late 1967 and 1968.

Also, consider Detroit newspaper circulation during the 1960s (see appendix, table 27). Both newspapers gained with the demise of the *Detroit Times* in 1960. The *News*, which bought the *Times* circulation list, saw its daily and Sunday circulation expand by more than 50 percent. However, both newspapers suffered losses in 1964 and 1968. Those losses were to be broadcasting's gain.

Although Detroit's television stations were not devoting the resources to news during the 1960s that they did during the 1970s or 1980s, they were making a start. WXYZ-TV, backed by the resources of the American Broadcasting Company, was about to challenge two competitors who had had the world of local Detroit television journalism to themselves for nearly two decades. WJBK-TV was using market research in an effort to guide its approach to news. Against this background, the biggest drama to hit the city since World War II, perhaps in the century, was about to develop.

4. A YEAR OF CHANGE

1967

The world of local television changed between 1960 and 1967. What happened during and after the week of July 23, 1967, however, was truly revolutionary not only for television but for metropolitan Detroit. That week saw the outbreak of the 1967 Detroit riot, also referred to as the 1967 Detroit insurrection. Had the riot occurred in 1963, Detroit television would certainly have covered it. But new technology allowed camera operators to do their work with more ease and to photograph for longer periods of time. Detroit's television commentators tried to provide a calming influence. But the pictures viewers saw were anything but soothing. The station that provided the most dramatic coverage, WXYZ-TV, drew a competitive advantage that it would hold for more than a decade.

These were straws in the wind. When WJR-AM newsman Phil Jones went on the air at 11:00 on Saturday night, July 22, 1967, he led the broadcast with a story about an earthquake in Turkey. Three stories followed about the country's simmering race problems.[1] News about Turkey and Vietnam was followed by a report about an insurrection in Birmingham, Alabama. Two hundred rioters had torn up the city's downtown business district, smashing car and store windows, Jones told listeners. A riot control tank was displayed to quiet the outbreak.[2] Jones told of a curfew in Youngstown, Ohio, after trouble there in which two buildings had been dynamited, a bar and a roller skating rink.[3] Jones reported that at a black power convention in Newark, New Jersey, attendees "began swinging fists and chairs" at newsmen interviewing conference delegates. Among other things, according to the *New York Times*, the group had called for "paramilitary training for Negro youths" and boycotting of "Negro publications accepting advertisements for hair straighteners and bleaching creams."[4]

Only blocks away at the WJBK-TV studios, newsman John Kelly reported both the Birmingham and Newark stories on the station's 11:00 p.m. Saturday newscast.[5] "CBS cameras were smashed, as were others. Newsmen escaped by jumping out of a window. One network engineer was kicked down a stairway," he reported.[6] Kelly then switched to a story about a National Guard honor ceremony at Camp Grayling during which Governor George Romney watched from the reviewing stand. Both Romney and the National Guard would be much in the news within twenty-four hours.

What neither Jones nor Kelly could have known was that the worst urban riot in post–World War II U.S. history was brewing within walking distance of their microphones. Jones could have seen its location from where he was sitting. An hour earlier, a policeman assigned to Detroit's vice squad had tried to buy a drink at an illegal establishment at Twelfth and Clairmount, where a party was in progress for two returning Vietnam veterans.[7] Detroit police finally crashed the party at 3:45 a.m. By 5:00 a.m., a full-blown riot was in progress, eventually claiming forty-three lives and causing $50 million in damage.

The story was made for television, with smoke, buildings in flames, tanks driving down once-peaceful streets, and a worried Detroit mayor Jerome P. Cavanagh and Governor Romney touring the smoking ruins of the city. But there was something else. Television, which made its debut before Detroit viewers in 1947, was a case of galloping technology. And that galloping technology galloped into the biggest story Detroit had seen since 1943, the city's last urban riot.

"We never had anything as dramatic as the riots in Detroit before that to really showcase the technology that we had. That was the first big test," recollected Mike Kalush, a WXYZ-TV news photographer between 1957 and 1999. Initially the cameras and power supplies used by television journalists were cumbersome, the dependability spotty. This had changed during the 1960s with the introduction of the Frezzolini battery, a power supply that allowed a camera to operate in the field for hours at a time. "Batteries really did change the way we think about things," said Kalush.[8] Cameras had become more portable by 1967 and could be perched on a camera operator's shoulders, something that would have been difficult to do previously. Film was faster, too, decreasing dependence on available light. Many observers believe that the power in Detroit media made the shift from print to electronic because of the riot. "It was so visual. And for the first time in their [television reporters] history, they had the equipment to tell a story visually. And they had the major story of that era," recalled Tom De Lisle, a former *Detroit Free Press* reporter who worked as a press secretary for Detroit mayor Roman S. Gribbs two and a half years after the riot.

It was probably the first story in local history that TV became as important, if not more important, than print media. We were getting immediate stuff from the TV—although obviously it had to be sent back and processed, it's not immediate like it is now. But for then—to put on Channel 7 and see these reports from all over town and fires going, and their people on the scene—it was so different. Newspapers are antiseptic—no matter how you look at it. It's not the same thing as seeing it. That riot, and the newspaper strike [of 1967–68] which followed, really opened the door for local TV. You could see it visually at press conferences—moving us not exactly aside, but bringing those guys up front . . . you could see the power shift going on.[9]

The power shift almost never happened, as Mayor Cavanagh implored the electronic press to withhold coverage of the riot. As it became clear that what was happening on Twelfth Street was something more than a minor insurrection, Cavanagh tried to suppress immediate coverage of the incident. WKNR-AM news director Phil Nye recalls getting an urgent message on the eighth hole of a West Bloomfield golf course that his station was trying to reach him. The message from the station was that Mayor Cavanagh wanted to talk.

I knew Jerry pretty well, on a first-name basis. [Newsman Bill] Bonds, Jerry, and I used to drink at the old Anchor Bar. He asked us not to air it [news of the Twelfth Street disturbance]. I was at the Bay Pointe Golf Club when I got a call about it. You could see the smoke from out there. And I told Jerry when he said, "You can't run it," I said, "My God, you've got thousands of people at Tiger Stadium and you've got the smoke plumes out in the air, and people are going to run toward it to see what the hell is going on if you don't warn them." . . . I didn't have much information when I talked to him at Bay Pointe. I said I wasn't going to make any decisions because I wasn't at the station. . . . I went back to the station and got as many facts together as I could. . . . Then I talked to Jerry and I said we were going to go with the story because of the people at Tiger Stadium. . . . He said, "You remember we had that little problem down on Kercheval. It ended. We think this is going to be the same way." I said, "It seems to me this is one hell of a lot bigger that what happened on Kercheval in 1966." And it was.[10]

WWJ-TV's James F. Clark remembered getting a call during the early morning hours from a *Detroit News* city editor to tell him that something serious was afoot. He sent reporter George Pruette to Twelfth and Clairmount, the center of the disturbance, and was ready to go with a newscast. However, Clark was ordered by WWJ-TV general manager James Schiavone not to air the film. Clark fumed, "How can you not talk about a riot? They're burning the damned town."[11]

The riot literally came to WJBK-TV's doorstep, but one visitor at the station on late Sunday afternoon had no sense of the insurrection until a rock came crashing through a station window. Marilyn Barnett was scheduled to perform a live commercial at WJBK-TV for the Farmer Jack grocery store chain. She sat in the station lobby with her two young children. "Rocks started to be thrown through the plate-glass windows at Channel 2. . . . I didn't know what was going on, or why," she recalls. "The intention was for them—the folks who were rioting—to take over the TV station."[12] Barnett and her children spent the night at Channel 2. (She got a police escort home early Monday morning.)

There was another problem facing Detroit's television newsrooms as they prepared to cover the biggest story in post–World War II Detroit history. The story was in Detroit's African American community, and the newsrooms had few connections in the streets of black Detroit.

Not only were there no African Americans employed in the newsrooms of Detroit's television stations, coverage of Detroit's African American community was spotty at best. "When I first started at [Channel] 7, they didn't put black people on the news," recalled Kalush. "I'm talking about covering black news in a black city—they didn't cover it. These little neighborhood groups would come up, these little protest groups—no one would ever give them any attention. That was just prior to the riot."[13]

Broadcast journalist Don Haney's career illustrates Kalush's point. As a young man growing up in Detroit during the 1950s, Haney dreamed of becoming a staff announcer on WJR-AM. But there were only one way to go for an African American broadcaster—to become a rhythm and blues deejay. "There was no variation in the career choice," Haney said. At the time, WJLB-AM was one of only a handful of places where African American deejays were heard. But Haney would not be deterred. He visited every station in Detroit, including WWJ-AM/TV. There, he was told by an executive: "You're a dammed fool for trying to get a job at a white station." Haney's response: "Instead of giving me a fit of depression, it spurred me on."[14]

Haney crossed the border in his effort to develop a career, finding work in Kitchener, London, and St. Thomas, Ontario. The Canadian Broadcasting Company picked up some of his work and aired it coast to coast. He would have stayed in Canada, but Haney's father, Mack, asked Haney to return home to run the family business—a funeral home on Detroit's east side. By 1964, the race barrier in Detroit radio had lowered somewhat, and Haney was hired at WJR-AM. By then Haney had a few friends in high places. A letter from Edward J. Robinson, executive director of the Archdiocese of Detroit's Community Affairs Department and an insider in the Cavanagh administration, requested that Cavanagh use his influence to get Haney a television job.[15] "As a negro he has experienced great difficulty in breaking into television," Robinson wrote Cavanagh. "I thought because of your relationship with Mr. Peter Clark [chief executive of the Evening News Association, which owned WWJ-TV] you might somehow arrange for a test for Mr. Haynie [sic] with WWJ-TV in hopes that we would eventually have some negro announcers or reporters on television in Detroit."[16] Cavanagh dispatched Anthony Ripley, a top aide who would later work as a *New York Times* reporter, to see what he could do. Ripley reported three weeks before the July 1967 riot: "Called Jim Clark (WWJ-TV's news director) at WWJ-TV—They had given him test, liked him, but he couldn't accept their offer."[17] Haney was hired later in 1967 by WXYZ-TV.

Jerry Blocker, who later became Detroit's first African American anchorman, faced similar problems. A Detroit native and 1949 graduate of Northwestern High School, Blocker had wanted to get into broadcasting from the time he was a child. But his mother warned him about trying to make in "in the white-folks field."[18]

Blocker found out the hard way that his mother was right. Following graduation from Wayne State University in 1953, he unsuccessfully auditioned at one Detroit radio station after another. "They put scripts in front of me that included nothing but classical music terms. Unless you know a lot about classical music, it's like reading in a foreign language. So I didn't do well."[19] Frustrated, Blocker sat out the 1950s working at an elementary school in Detroit's Cass Corridor.

The owners of WCHD-FM (now WCHB-FM) finally hired Blocker in 1960. WWJ-TV brought Blocker in for an interview after the 1967 Detroit riots. Many guessed that WWJ-TV's hiring of Blocker had something to do with the ugly reality that Detroit television had no African American reporters to cover a changing Detroit. But the speculation wasn't altogether true. WWJ-TV executives could read U.S. Census Bureau reports as well as anybody, and knew the time had come to break the station's on-air racial barrier. News director Jim Clark lunched often with Al Dunmore, managing editor of the *Michigan Chronicle*, Detroit's African American weekly. Dunmore suggested Blocker for a newsroom post.[20]

Blocker recalled, "We didn't know how I was going to be accepted by blacks or whites. It was quite a gamble . . . none of this came easy. The social and financial realities finally seeped their way up to the top management."[21] That was later, however. A large reality—a major insurrection—was about to hit Detroit and its television medium.

Detroit's 1967 riot was, at once, both more and less difficult to cover than one might imagine. Most reporters recalled that they felt little sense of physical danger from rioters. According to William Serrin, part of the *Detroit Free Press* team that won a Pulitzer Prize for the newspaper, "I came to the *Free Press* in 1966, March 1966. This was obviously a segregated town. But you could go to black clubs as a white person. There was a lot of intermingling, [although] there was still a separation. You could go to a jazz club. When the riot started, I—and, I think, a lot of others—didn't feel any trepidation at all. I went down to Twelfth Street that morning. I didn't feel any qualms about going down there."[22] De Lisle recalls answering the telephone at the *Detroit Free Press* newsroom: "They [the callers] were kind of looking to us for help and asking questions about what was going on, and how bad was it and how long was it going to last. What used to amaze me, as a copyboy going into homes asking for pictures of somebody who had died, how people respond to you like you're an authority figure, even though you're just a newspaperman."[23]

Kalush remembers arriving at Twelfth and Clairmount by 11:00 a.m. "It was sort of a carnival atmosphere at the time. Nobody had any idea what would be involved. Everybody was having a pretty good time at that point. There was a lot of looting going on, crazy things like that. But there wasn't any real hatred."[24]

Kalush and reporter Jim Herrington toured the area, largely unharassed. "The black folks in town just loved Jim," said Kalush. "We didn't have any kind of racial confrontation at all that first day."[25] Kerner Commission investigators later noted "the carefree mood with which people ran in and out of stores, looting and laughing, and joking with the police officers" during the first day of the disturbance.[26]

"They allowed me to be an impartial observer," said Ira Rosenberg, a *Detroit Free Press* photographer. "Working alone in all of the areas, twenty-four hours a day, I was never attacked or threatened in any way. . . . Both sides, the police and the blacks, seemed to accept us." He added that Detroit police, in fact, were cooperative. "If there was something happening that they knew we didn't know about, somebody would say, 'Hey, look over on this street. They're doing this or that.'" He further remembered that he "left my camera on top of my car on a side street, by mistake. I came running back. There was a young black man standing by the car—I had the press sign in the window. He saw me running up. I came up and he says, 'It's alright. I was watching your camera. . . . He didn't grab the camera—which was a Leika, worth hundreds of dollars."[27]

As researchers later noted about the riot coverage in general, the "tone of the coverage was predominately calm and 'factual' as opposed to 'emotional' and excitive.'"[28] Viewers received box scores. How many fires had been started during the previous twenty-four hours? How many arrests? How many shootings? How many deaths?

Local news cameramen, indeed, did their jobs. As investigators studied television coverage in Detroit, Newark, Cincinnati, and Tampa, they tallied nine looting scenes that made the national airwaves. Seven of those scenes were caught in Detroit. Half the scenes of rioters wielding firearms originated from Detroit.

But the ease with which reporters mingled with rioters changed on Monday night, the second night of the riot. A sniper on Detroit's east side had gunned down a young fireman, Carl E. Smith, as he arrived to fight a blaze.[29] WXYZ-TV showed a shot of the fireman's boots near the operating table, along with images of bloodied people in the emergency room. "There was terror on both sides."[30]

By almost every analysis, WXYZ-TV distinguished itself by being on the street, where the action was. As reporter Herrington recalled, "The other stations were showing the official stuff—news conferences, white guys sitting around tables. We were out there."[31] There are various reasons why WJBK-TV and WWJ-TV were beaten on the story. One was a sense of disbelief that the riot had occurred at all. This was illustrated by an analysis delivered Tuesday night, the third night of the riot, by Robert McBride, WJBK-TV's director of news and public affairs. He had influence, if not control, of what aired on the station's airwaves. An archconservative, McBride looked at the riot with a sense of incredulity, believing that the insurrection could only have been caused by malcontents and/or outside agitation. He called the battle something that had been waged by "a small group of die-hard extremists in the Negro community, some of them undoubtedly from out of town." He went on to say:

> All during the past three days, there have been rumors that this violence was planned weeks ago, that various extremist action groups have been plotting it.
>
> Two facts tonight make these rumors believable: First, the Negro man-in-the-street and his family don't like the violence. They are the ones being hurt by it. Detroit officials won't talk about it publicly, but they know about terrorist groups who have fomented trouble here before. Negro leaders in Detroit know about these extremist Negro organizations, too; they don't like them, but say they can't do much to force them to change their tactics.[32]

Another factor made the coverage more difficult. Whom to interview? "By the second or third day it was hard to get anybody to talk, except for a few," Kalush later recalled. "Most of the good people were hiding, and the people that were out were the people looking for trouble. I know this now in hindsight, I didn't know this at the time: A lot of folks spent their days on the floor in their house, scared to death."[33] Rosenberg remembered meeting a woman on the street, and how he shot one of his most memorable photographs. According to Rosenberg, she asked: "'Do you want to see how I got through these riots?' Guess what? I got a picture of her sitting in the bathtub reading a book. She said, 'I felt that was the safest place to be.'"[34]

Missing from the reportage was any explanation of the causes of the riot. How did the country's fifth-largest city erupt into a hellfire of flames, bullets, and looting? There was little mention of the new freeways that had destroyed African American communities and shoehorned their residents into already-cramped neighborhoods, or the discriminatory practices of landlords, storeowners, and business executives. Later, the *Detroit Free*

Press sent a team of investigators to examine each of the forty-three riot deaths. The reporters concluded that most of the deaths were caused by frightened Michigan National Guard troops firing wildly at anything that moved.

As De Lisle pointed out, the story was made for television. It was visual. Viewers saw numerous shots of angry people, looters crawling through broken shop windows, and fires consuming building after building. But two scenes were repeated over and over again on the air, one of which confirmed the worst stereotypes held by white Detroiters, the other a symbol of what was to come. WXYZ-TV reporter Jim Herrington interviewed one looter, a middle-aged, grossly overweight African American woman who was taking dresses from a store through a broken window and holding them to her chest in an attempt to size the clothing. "She was only going to take the ones that fit," according to Kalush. "We kind of moseyed on up to her. Jim stuck the microphone in her face."[35] The exchange went as follows:

Herrington: Do you think there's anything wrong with what you're doing here?

Woman: No, it's going to burn anyways. And I could use a new dress.

Herrington: What do you think about all this?

Woman: I think it's kind of all awful. . . . All the stores are closed, and the restaurants . . .

Herrington: Do you blame anybody?

Woman: I don't know who to blame.[36]

The scene could easily be construed as a stereotypical example of African Americans wanting something for nothing, painting the riot as nothing more than a shopping spree.

It was Kalush who shot a sequence that, in many ways, would symbolize what was going to happen to the city. The shot was of a woman driving north on Woodward Avenue. She had a pistol in her hand, draped over her steering wheel. "I was scared to death. . . . I thought she'd shoot me. She didn't even hardly look at me. She looked like was in a trance. She was terrified." Another image was of a Caucasian burning his own store and running out the back door. "I can still see that guy running out the back door, with smoke coming out the front," said Kalush.[37]

But the key to WXYZ-TV's coverage was Bill Bonds's anchoring abilities. Bonds had always believed in infusing the news with drama, with his personality. Here was the most dramatic story of his lifetime, and his personality showed through. It was "his [Bonds's] finest hour. I could say it's been downhill since then. I thought he demonstrated in 1967, and he was the only one who did so among the electronic reporters, a real compassion for the city, and a real hurt to see the city in flames. And he communicated that. I think that's what endeared him to so many people," said Coleman A. Young, a state senator during the 1967 insurrection. "He showed a compassion, an understanding of the city that nobody else showed."[38]

"They'd just had enough," noted Kalush. "It was not just one thing. It was a bunch of things—not being able to get good jobs, not being able to get on the police force, not being able to get to be a fireman, not being able to be a mail carrier. I think it was an accumulation of a ton of things. It just came to a head."[39]

In an editorial, WJBK-TV officials opined, "It is most necessary that the man in the street with the problem be the first person to be asked about the problem. Only in this way can the true depth of the problem be known and an effective solution be worked out."[40] In a July 30, 1967, documentary, WWJ-TV characterized the insurrection as "a chaotic and irrational collection of fires, crime and blind anger."[41]

Critiquing the television coverage, *Detroit Free Press* television critic Bettelou Peterson wrote, "Detroit broadcasters have kept calm and tried to keep their audience that way."[42] *Detroit News* television and radio writer Frank Judge felt that "in contrast to experiences in some other cities—especially Los Angeles during the burning of Watts—the coverage has been calm throughout. There has been a complete absence of the hysterical or racially inciting approach."[43]

WWJ-TV faced another obstacle: theft of valuable film footage. More than three decades after the fact, station veterans are still rankled by how NBC News producers stole footage from the station's newsroom. Reporter Riley groused:

The NBC guy—producer, runner, gopher, whoever the hell he was—found out the route, the system, and he intercepted the film. Instead of getting a copy—he didn't want to waste time, of course—so he sent the goddamn film to NBC. And we lost most of our fire coverage. . . . The NBC guys were getting nothing. That was probably the reason this happened. NBC didn't know where to go, they didn't know the town, they didn't know the city. They were always a day late and a dollar short. So what to do? Steal our stuff. That just put a great big hole in our coverage. You didn't know what was happening. You'd say, "Where's the gas station fire?" Well, we didn't know. It was here. It was there. It must be in the projection. Then, it was forgotten about.[44]

And there was little mention of the Michigan National Guard's performance during the riot. Seemingly all of the newsmen involved in the coverage knew that the guardsmen were shooting recklessly at everything that moved. WWJ-TV's Riley recalled touring a burglarized ROTC facility with Detroit police when shots crashed through a nearby window. It was a National Guardsman who had seen movement in the building and opened fire. The movement, of course, was only Riley and a few Detroit policemen. Asked why he never mentioned what he and everybody else knew, Riley said it had a lot to do with the social mores of reporting. "We didn't want to make the National Guard look bad, because they were in there . . . to help. Today, of course, that would maybe be a front-page article, a sidebar—'National Guard Scared to Death.' . . . Just like drinking with the mayor: we didn't talk about that stuff. Why the hell didn't the newsmen in the White House report Kennedy always screwing around? That wasn't the thing then. You just didn't do that."[45]

Perhaps this was beside the point. What John F. Day had written in 1958 about the power of television news, its ability to catapult viewers "onto the field of action," had become true in a big way.[46] Hundreds of thousands of viewers watched the burning and the looting. Whether or not the television reporters had conveyed their stories with a sense of calm made no difference. Television had brought the Detroit insurrection into their homes. Bonds delivered the news emotionally, with personality. Within a year, he was promoted to an anchor job at KABC-TV, the ABC-owned television station in Los Angeles. The job was in a bigger city and paid more money.

However, whatever goodwill WXYZ-TV had built up was gone. "After the riots it got so bad that we couldn't even drive our car through the neighborhood without getting stoned. . . . We took all of our cars to Earl Scheib [an automotive body painting concern] and had them painted. . . . That lasted, I would say, six months before we could actually go into a neighborhood and identify ourselves as a news crew," Kalush later recalled. "The black community felt we were prejudiced. I don't think they cared for media people at all after the riot."[47]

WWJ-TV's dominance evaporated with the smoke of the riot. Reporter Riley later recalled that "after the riot, we were no longer the station to turn to for news. We held onto footage while Channel 7 interrupted every few minutes with new film. They showed every damned thing, even unedited stuff."[48]

Although Arbitron did not segment out television viewership during the week of the insurrection, WJBK-TV and WWJ-TV clearly did well. WXYZ-TV was no longer merely a blip on the radar screen (see appendix, table 28).

There might be another interpretation: WJBK-TV and WXYZ-TV understood the dramatic potential of the riot while the other stations did not. But an even bigger change was about to hit local television—by way of New York City and Chicago.

The world of local Detroit television news changed even further on November 16, 1967. On that evening, Local 372 of the International Brotherhood of Teamsters struck *The Detroit News*. The *Detroit Free Press* locked out its employees, closing both of Detroit's major daily newspapers. By the time the labor dispute ended nearly nine months later, in August 1968, the disagreement had mushroomed into the country's longest newspaper blackout.[49] The work stoppage was only the latest in the acid relations between Detroit's dailies and unions representing workers at both businesses. A similar dispute in 1964 closed both dailies for 134 days between July and November. At that time, it was the lengthiest newspaper strike in the country's history.[50]

The strike, of course, left Detroiters without key sources of information at a crucial time in the country's history. While the newspapers were shuttered, two major political leaders (Martin Luther King Jr. and Robert F. Kennedy) were assassinated, President Lyndon Johnson announced that he would not be running for reelection, and the Vietnam War increased in intensity, as did antiwar activity. Both Cavanagh and George Romney made unsuccessful attempts to end the strike. The combination of turbulent times and absence of newspapers proved to be an unhealthy one. The rumor mill kicked into high gear. "The hysteria is awful," Detroit police commissioner Ray Girardin told the *New York Times*. "Whites, for example, talk about Negro plans to set fires on expressways by rolling gasoline drums onto the roads, or sending killer squads to invade suburbs and murder children. Negroes talk about white plans to provoke racial incidents and then invade Negro neighborhoods in the city."[51] The strike was a great opportunity for Detroit's television stations to step into the vacuum. "Nobody thought we could put on a newscast without the newspapers, given the amount of information we borrowed," explained Jim Herrington, "but we managed to pull it off."[52]

Immediately after the strike began, a group of *Detroit Free Press* reporters contacted Wayne State University about producing a television news program on WTVS-TV, Detroit's public television station. The Ford Foundation, with encouragement from former CBS News president Fred W. Friendly, anted up $40,000 for the project.[53] *Television City Room* featured *Detroit Free Press* television critic Bettelou Peterson reviewing television, sports columnist Joe Falls broadcasting sports, and reporter/editor Nickie McWhirter covering news. The program lasted ten weeks before the money ran out and the venture was abandoned.

One television personality who capitalized on the strike was WKBD-TV interviewer Lou Gordon, who hosted a weekly public affairs show on the station from 1965 until his death in 1977 from a heart attack. Gordon's show was "must" viewing for anybody interested in metro Detroit public life. He went after public officials and large companies that he felt abused the public's trust. Michigan governor George Romney, who once walked off his show, was a favorite target.

Gordon, a native Detroiter, served in the U.S. Army Air Corps (later the Air Force) during World War II. Upon discharge, he went into journalism and received his training in one of the craft's tougher battlefields. Silliman Evans Sr., publisher of the *Nashville Tennessean*, needed a reporter to cover Memphis and the political machine of E. H. "Boss" Crump—one of the state's most feared powerbrokers. Crump, a Memphis businessman, had controlled the state's Democratic Party for nearly fifty years. Covering

Crump was not an easy assignment, since reporters with the job sometimes ended up in jail. Gordon signed on.

It was a great story. Nobody knew it at the time, but Crump's kingdom was crumbling. Estes Kefauver, a four-term congressman, was running for a seat in the U.S. Senate—very much against Crump's wishes. Crump took out an ad in newspapers likening Kefauver to a tricky raccoon. Kefauver thereupon donned a coonskin cap, remarking: "I may be a pet coon, but I'll never be Mr. Crump's pet coon."[54] Kefauver whipped the seemingly invincible Crump machine and won the election, going on to a quarter-century career in the U.S. Senate and two presidential candidacies. Gordon later worked with muckraker Drew Pearson, but cut short his journalism career in the early 1950s.[55] Gordon's father fell ill, requiring Gordon's return to Detroit to run the family business.

For years, Gordon had two jobs: by day, he was a middleman for a women's clothing manufacturer. By night, he exercised his zeal for journalism. He hosted *Lou Gordon's Hotseat* on WXYZ-TV and WXYZ-AM, and later took his work to WKBD-TV. Gordon was an old-fashioned populist. After his death in 1977, his widow, Jackie, read a tribute from an unnamed viewer. "Lou was always at the forefront in the battle for justice, peace and quality," wrote the fan. "He took on the warmongers, the bigots, the crooks and the moneygrubbers with equal fervor. He was the voice of our conscience, and he spoke for the voiceless and the powerless—for the victims of injustice, war and corruption."[56]

Gordon was famous for leading crusades against big utility companies, including Michigan Bell. He would hammer Governor George Romney, Detroit mayor Jerome P. Cavanagh, and just about anybody in a position of power. He went after former Detroit mayor Louis Miriani about suspicious campaign contributions. (Miriani was later jailed on tax evasion charges.) The national guests were impressive: Ralph Nader, former Alabama governor George Wallace, NBC News anchorman Chet Huntley, and *Hustler* magazine publisher Larry Flynt. Gordon mixed in transsexuals, pimps, and reputed Mafia hit men—just to keep things interesting. (Upon Gordon's death, a who's who of Michigan politicians delivered assessments of Gordon. The list included a sitting U.S. senator (Donald Riegle), a future U.S. senator (Carl Levin), lawyer F. Lee Bailey, and Governor William Milliken, who said: "His bold brand of journalism challenged comfortable assumptions. He kept many of us alert to divergent viewpoints."[57]

It was on Gordon's show in 1967 that Michigan governor George Romney, at the time a serious presidential candidate, said he had been "brainwashed" on the topic of Vietnam. Romney was roundly ridiculed for using the word and forced out of the presidential race, which was later won by Richard Nixon. It is worth examining a transcript of the October 31, 1967, broadcast, if only because Romney's comments seem so mild in retrospect. Missing also is the usual Gordon bravado.

Gordon: Governor, shifting to Vietnam. In November of 1965, when you returned from Vietnam, you said—and I'm quoting: "Involvement was morally right and necessary, and probably reversed the shift in the balance of power greater than if Hitler had conquered Europe." In recent weeks, you said you didn't think we should have been involved at all, and that President Johnson's decision to expand the bombing wasn't going to resolve the problem. Isn't your position a bit inconsistent with what it was? And what do you propose we do now?

Romney: Well, you know when I came back from Vietnam I had just had the greatest brainwashing that anybody can get? When you . . .

Gordon: By the generals?

Romney: Not only by the generals, but also by the diplomatic corps over there. They do a very thorough job. Since returning from Vietnam I've gone into the history of Vietnam all the way back into World War II and before. And, as a result, I have changed my mind in that particular. I no longer believe that it was necessary for us to get involved in South Vietnam to stop Communist aggression in Southeast Asia, and to prevent Communist domination—I mean Chinese Communist domination—of Southeast Asia. And I've indicated that I think it was tragic that we became involved in the conflict there. If General Eisenhower had remained president of the United States, I don't think we would have become involved in a land war in Southeast Asia. But despite that fact, we are there. We are involved. We have created this into a conflict that is now a test between Communism and freedom there. And this is part of the complexity and difficulty of the situation. And furthermore, we've involved other nations in Southeast Asia, and we have to deal with it on the basis of the current circumstances, rather than on what might have been if there hadn't been an overreaction—in military terms—in dealing with the Vietnamese problem."[58]

Although Gordon's usual pugnacity is lacking, his flair for publicity was in full flower. Jeanne Findlater, a producer on Gordon's show, said later that Gordon saw to it that the media was alerted after the statement.

> We always looked for ways to promote the show. So we got the studio audiotape. I racked it up and I called UPI and AP and a third one. I had three phones in our office hanging over the back of a chair. I had a little tape recorder player and I racked the thing up. I said to each of the desks, "You know I have Governor Romney on the *Lou Gordon Show* tonight, you might want to hear this"—which they did. I had to keep playing it over and over again while they took it down because they were taking it down from the tape recorder—three receivers hanging over the back of the chair. . . . It hurt him in his bid for the presidency and I'll never understand why. I thought it was so typical of his honorableness that he was so forthright. I always felt terrible about my role in that.[59]

Each of the news organizations carried stories. Romney's nascent presidential campaign never recovered. And Detroit television claimed its first political victim.

Until the 1960s, television had been unable to capitalize on its video capabilities and its dramatic potential. That changed. Now, partly by default, partly by changing conditions, partly because of newspaper labor problems, Detroit television had a seat at the civic table. News also assumed a more important place in the television industry. News had been a money loser, an item that was not as important as revenue-producing entertainment programming. That, too, was about to change in a major way.

Television news presentation had been dull and straightforward throughout the 1950s and most of the 1960s. What would be considered "show business" elements were studiously avoided, as a gulf remained between the world of journalism and the world of entertainment. The idea of making news entertaining had been breached on the television network level, primarily by NBC anchorman David Brinkley, who injected wit and wry humor into the mix. During the late 1960s, that gulf between "entertainment" and "news" would be bridged, as cosmetic and personality elements were introduced. Form and style were becoming more important than substance. And news, previously a money loser, was about to become a moneymaker. With local television broadcasts getting bigger audiences, advertisers became more interested.

The late 1960s saw a total overhaul in local television news presentation. The ABC-owned stations led the change, turning William S. Paley's original mission on its head. Paley had said he believed in hiring based on journalistic skill. The chiefs of the ABC stations, however, based hiring on personality and television skill. Paley had sought respectability for the new medium of radio. ABC sought revenue because the financial performance of the owned television stations division was critical to the success of the company. As ABC chairman Leonard Goldenson later related, the ABC Television Network lost roughly $120 million between 1961 and 1971. The loss was financed by the company's theater operations. "As that part of our business dwindled," wrote Goldenson, "the money to continue network operations came from profits earned at the company-owned stations."[1]

The best way to increase revenue, ABC executives believed, was to drive the company's news departments to number one in each of its five markets. They held that programming leadership automatically followed news leadership. To achieve that, they introduced a "personality" element into news. "In news, the [ABC-owned] television stations pioneered the introduction of a human element to lessen the formality of news presentations," the company's corporate officers wrote in a 1975 annual report.[2] This is exactly what Bonds did during the Detroit riots, about the same time that ABC embarked on its new corporate mission.

Richard O'Leary, the station group president, succinctly described the ABC-owned station news philosophy. O'Leary, as general manager of WLS-TV in Chicago, had hired veteran Chicago anchorman Fahey Flynn away from that city's CBS-owned station. O'Leary also brought in anchorman Joel Daly from Cleveland's NBC-owned TV operation. This is how O'Leary explained the duo's order of battle:

> For example, there's a train wreck. Flynn gives the main headline, "ten people killed." Instead of pausing for a commercial before giving details, he takes it to conclusion. Then he says, 'something is wrong here, Joel. There are too many damned train wrecks and equipment failures.' And Joel Daly reacts to this. He might follow with a sidebar story but the main thing was reacting, because this is spontaneous, not scripted. It's Flynn daringly set free to say whatever comes to his mind to Joel or to the weatherman, the sports man, or the reporter. By stepping outside the traditional role of reading the news, their personalities come across. . . . We are not dealing with mere news, we are dealing with information and in people.[3]

O'Leary's vision was revolutionary. Journalism would no longer be "mere news." It would be "information" and "people." The man who executed O'Leary's vision better than any other television executive is Albert T. Primo, who is widely, but perhaps inaccurately, credited with the development of what later became known as "Happy Talk" in New York City.[4] "Happy Talk" is the practice of television news personalities conversing or joking during a newscast. Curiously, that was not at all what Primo originally had in mind when he became a television executive.

Primo had been news director at Philadelphia's KYW-TV. While there, he discovered a clause in the station's union contract that stated anybody could report a story. As he later related to author Ron Powers, a Pulitzer Prize–winning television critic for the *Chicago Sun-Times:* "I tried to find the guy who had the most contacts at city hall, and he became the city hall reporter. Another guy had medical space interest; he became a science reporter. There was a labor reporter, a transportation reporter."[5] He had also importuned the on-air personalities at KYW-TV to interact with each other, a recommendation made by McHugh and Hoffman. The journalism was good, the television was a refreshing change, and ratings went up. ABC officials noted his success and hired him at WABC-TV, the ABC-owned station in New York. When he arrived in September 1968 as director of news and public affairs, WABC's ratings were not good. Its 11:00 p.m. ratings were less than half of those at WNBC-TV or WCBS-TV, respectively the NBC-owned and CBS-owned television stations in New York. WABC-TV had a 6 rating, meaning 6 percent of the television sets in New York City metropolitan area were tuned to the station's late newscast. WNBC-TV and WCBS-TV earned 15 and 13 ratings during those same periods.[6] By 1970, after Primo and WABC-TV introduced a new set of broadcast techniques labeled *Eyewitness News*, WABC-TV and WNBC-TV were tied with 12 ratings, with WCBS-TV earning an 11 rating.

To understand why the ratings were so important at the network-owned stations in New York, one must look at the financial picture of each of the networks. Each of the three television networks owned five stations. ABC, as previously mentioned, owned television outlets in New York, Los Angeles, Chicago, San Francisco, and Detroit. CBS owned stations in New York, Los Angeles, Chicago, Philadelphia, and St. Louis. NBC owned stations in New York, Los Angeles, Chicago, Washington, DC, and Cleveland.

As table 29 illustrates (see appendix), the network owned-station division made more money than the networks themselves until 1972. In 1970 the owned-station division made double the profits the networks themselves made. One can safely assume that revenue from the country's largest advertising market would be of vital importance to the networks.

At first, as *New York Times* television critic John J. O'Connor later wrote, the early efforts were "enough to trigger automatic smiles of condescension, especially among journalists in and out of television, whose concepts of news were firmly grounded in the traditions of print."[7]

Primo's new technique, heavily promoted by O'Leary, involved human interaction among the newscasters, reporters, weathercasters, and sportscasters. Primo's success made him something of a legend in the broadcast industry.

Independently, however, the technique was already in the process of being developed at Detroit's WJBK-TV in 1965. The station that year hired Jerry Hodak, a twenty-three-year-old Detroit native. Noting Hodak's youth and nervousness, a station executive recommended to anchors Jac Le Goff and John Kelly that they joke with Hodak on the air to settle him down. "He [WJBK-TV program director Dean McCarthy] suggested that we tease him [Hodak] a little bit to help make him feel comfortable and loosen up," wrote Kelly.[8] As Hodak later commented on Le Goff and Kelly:

> John and Jac were totally irreverent and without mercy. They called me "Geraldine" and made fun of my blazers. I assumed it was all their idea, because it was entirely in keeping with their characters. There was John's laugh. . . . He was just naturally funny. During the first commercial break in our debut, one of the station managers at the time, Jay Watson, told us to get on with the show and cut out the bullshit. Within the first hour after we got off the air, the "bullshit" drew 400 calls into the station from the viewers at home. The folks at home didn't know what to make of it, but they knew we were having a good time.[9]

The new technique did not yet have a name, but Happy Talk in Detroit television was born. A case can be made that Detroit was the birthplace of Happy Talk. WJBK-TV's research consultant, McHugh and Hoffman, Inc., encouraged the practice. "Measures should be taken to reinstate the 'team feeling' during all TV2 newscasts. Verbal transitions between Le Goff and Kelly, et al, should be encouraged, and a closing team shot of all the members interacting with one another should be included," advised the firm. But not all forms of chitchat would do. McHugh and Hoffman also advised: "Caution should be exercised in order to prevent 'in-studio' humor between news team members. It has been noticed that lately, [there is a] tendency for 'in-crowd' type jokes between the men, leaving the viewer wondering what is so funny. This should not be allowed to happen, as viewer identification with the news team cannot be sacrificed."[10]

The Detroit innovation was not widely noticed throughout the broadcast industry. That notice went to New York City's WABC-TV under Primo, where some of the same elements were used, but with flourishes. The news team related to each other on the air. They joked. Anchorman Roger Grimsby often made sly sexual innuendoes, referring to sex as "horizontal enrichment." Grimsby, fellow anchorman Bill Beutel, weathercaster Tex Antoine, and sportscaster Jim Bouton joked constantly. The *Times*'s

O'Connor noted: "In terms of news content, 'Eyewitness News' is not, except for a more personal bias, much different from its electronic competitors. In terms of television, it is way out in front—and not only in the ratings."[11]

WABC-TV was also in front in another way—the way it promoted its journalistic product. The late 1960s and early 1970s also saw the development of advertising techniques to sell newscasters, with many of those techniques being developed at ABC-owned stations. WABC-TV had previously run advertisements promoting the team members as if they were family. They were shown "playing football together in Central Park, dining together, playing cards, reading fan letters and attending a Puerto Rican wedding party."[12] The station's reporters became local celebrities. The news team was not a group of journalists bringing news to viewers. It was a happy, chortling family that came into your home to entertain. As O'Leary had said, this was not about "mere" news. It was about information and people. That was the way the news team was sold to viewers.

Part of the *Eyewitness News* formula involved broadening ethnic representation in television newsrooms. The same was happening in Detroit. Among the first African American reporters to appear on Detroit television was Bob Bennett. An Indianapolis native, Bennett came to Detroit in 1962 as a newsman and gospel disc jockey for WCHB-AM. WWJ-TV tried to hire Bennett in the mid-1960s, but his supervisors at WCHB-AM boosted his salary by $50 a week. He moved to WXYZ-AM in 1965, and was wooed by WXYZ-TV.[13] However, WWJ-TV also continued to court Bennett and signed him in May 1968. At the time he was the station's second black reporter. (The first was Jerry Blocker.) Bennett worked five days a week at WWJ-TV while doing news on WWJ-AM on Saturdays. He broke the story of the 1969 arrest of John Norman Collins, a suspect in the sensational co-ed serial murders in the Ann Arbor area. Print and broadcast journalists alike viewed him as one of the best reporters in Detroit. "I think he's one of the deans of local television news," said MSNBC's Mike Huckman.[14]

The respect for Bennett extended to city hall. Former Detroit City Council president Gil Hill was a policeman when he got to know Bennett in the 1960s. "You know how cops are about reporters," comments Hill. "They don't like to say much. But nobody ever had any hesitation about talking to Bob Bennett. He was unfailingly fair and accurate, never violated a confidence and never took a cheap shot. I don't know of anybody who said they were screwed by Bob Bennett. And you can't say that about many reporters."[15]

WXYZ-TV hired Doris Biscoe in 1973. She was educated at Washington, DC's Howard University and worked in Washington in radio and as a model (she is five feet, eleven inches) before pursuing a television career. A relative of hers, former Wayne County sheriff William Lucas, suggested to WXYZ-TV news director Phil Nye that he take a look at Biscoe's audition tape. "He told me, 'Look, I don't know if she's got it or not, but I'd appreciate it if you at least give her a look,'" Nye recalls.[16] After signing on as a reporter on WXYZ-TV's late news, Biscoe anchored the station's 6:00 p.m., noon, and early morning newscasts.

The broadening of ethnic representation took place in many ABC-owned station newsrooms. For instance, WABC-TV's Primo hired a young lawyer with no journalistic experience and turned him into a reporter. Geraldo Rivera, of Puerto Rican and Jewish descent, was a lawyer representing disadvantaged New Yorkers when he was hired at WABC. Primo also hired Rose Ann Scamardella, who had been an unpaid member of a municipal board but had no journalistic experience. She was, however, unmistakably Italian. The station hired Melba Tolliver, a secretary of African American descent at ABC who got her first on-air experience while ABC reporters were on strike. She had been trained as a nurse, later attending a New York University journalism training seminar for one summer. One can look at this in two ways. One was the way longtime ABC News executive Av Westin saw it. He called it a "blatant case of playing to the audience." Westin compared WABC-TV's hiring practice to the "Three I" game played by New York City politicians. As Westin pointed out, politicians balanced their election tickets "by picking an *I*talian, *I*rishman, and a Jew (*I*sraelite)."[17] Another way of looking at the new hiring practice was that New York's local television newsrooms were beginning to look more like the city of New York. Even Rivera, a beneficiary of the new system, later cynically admitted that his hiring had everything to do with ethnicity and nothing to do with journalism. As he told *Chicago Sun-Times* critic Ron Powers, "One day Gloria Rojas [a WABC reporter] called me up and said that ABC was looking for a Puerto Rican. Just like that. I mean, she didn't pull any punches. She wasn't kidding around. I mean, I had no experience, so obviously they didn't want me for that. They had an ethnic slot available."[18]

All of these reporters distinguished themselves journalistically in some way. As Westin himself pointed out, "[T]o her credit, Scamardella recognized that her experience was limited, and she moved to correct her inadequacies. She worked hard in an on-the-job training program."[19] Rivera was later lauded for his reporting about the Willowbrook State School, a Staten Island institution with what was characterized as "one of the largest institutions for the mentally retarded in the world." Rivera went in unannounced one morning with a crew and recorded patients under "uncontrolled" conditions.[20]

The station also began using news consultants to suggest changes in the product. Consultants usually traveled from city to city, or "market" to "market," as they would say. They were trained in research, psychology, and audience appeal techniques. As Harvey Gersin, who had worked as a consultant for WXYZ-TV explained, "[W]e study viewer psychology. Based on that, we develop a strategy for our client—appearance of the set, writing, special content, features, interrelationship of talent on the set."[21] They were not trained, however, as journalists.

As weatherman Jerry Hodak later remarked: "What had really started to happen . . . was that local news had become very popular, and the revenues generated from it started to grow. It became an issue of economics. The station that could capture the larger audience share could sell its ad spots for a higher rate and would have a head start on prime time viewers in the bargain."[22] At that point, news was too important to be left to the journalists. Sales specialists were brought in to sell it. Market researchers were brought in to shape it as a program. However, network news executives pointedly turned up their noses at such techniques. CBS News president Richard S. Salant, who ran CBS News for all but three years between 1961 and 1979, thought that using consultants was an abandonment of a station executive's responsibilities.

As planned, the five ABC-owned stations made a blatant grab for the top broadcast personalities in each of its five television markets. "We would go in and simply offer to double somebody's salary if we thought they could do us good," recalled Phil Nye, who oversaw news at the five ABC-owned stations during the 1970s.[23] In Los Angeles, KABC-TV hired Jerry Dunphy, a longtime anchorman from the Los Angeles CBS station. "Jerry's defection from 'The Big News' on 2 to 'Eyewitness News' on 7 changed the face of local television news viewing in L.A. to this day," wrote Dennis Swanson, a former KABC-TV news director.[24] In Chicago, ABC's WLS-TV hired longtime anchorman Flynn away from CBS's WBBM-TV.

The money was enormous. "ABC was making so much money Leonard Goldenson did not know what to do with it," explained Nye. He remembers being ordered in 1978 to spend money, and getting a 10 percent bonus simply because "nobody knew what else to do with the money."[25]

A look at the balance sheet of the American Broadcasting Companies shows an upward spiral of both revenue and net income. The company did not segregate the financial operations of its various properties. The company's network television operations, for instance, obviously dramatically impacted the company's financial operations. There are hints about the financial rewards of a first-place finish in news ratings. The *New York Times* wrote in 1974 that first-place KGO-TV, the ABC-owned station in San Francisco, commanded $900 for a thirty-second commercial. The figure was triple what the station's competitors charged.[26] Year after year, the company's annual reports described record revenue and net income at its owned television station division. The company repeatedly asserted that the group was "the most successful group of owned stations in the nation, both in terms of earned revenue and in programming leadership.[27] The company's net income doubled between 1970 and 1972, doubled again by 1977, and almost doubled again by 1979.

As table 30 shows (see appendix), ABC's net income increased almost ninefold during the decade. The company, in its various annual reports, said that the five-station division reported record revenues and net income in 1973, 1976, and 1979. By way of comparison, Storer Broadcasting had less of an emphasis on news. None of its annual reports of the era mention news, as did the annual reports of the American Broadcasting Company. Although there are many factors involved in a television station's profitability, it is clear that Storer, although not hurting for money, was not performing as well (see appendix, table 31).

Numbers such as ABC's, and WABC's success, caused television stations to change the way they did business. Most of the changes were made in the presentation, not necessarily the content. In Chicago, the ABC-owned station experimented with a similar personalization of the news. In this case, it again sold the news team as "just folks." For instance, it turned out that WLS-TV anchorman Joel Daly, a magna cum laude graduate of Yale University, liked country music. He wrote country music songs and sang them at festivals, showing viewers that he was an "average" guy—despite the Yale University degree. At San Francisco's KGO-TV, the results were even more dramatic. The station evolved a form of newscast that was so saturated with sex and violence that local wags joked the station's call letters stood for "Kicks, Guts, and Orgasms." *60 Minutes*' Mike Wallace reported on the station's newscasts in 1974, noting that some 55 percent of the station's news content during one week in January 1974 was devoted to crime and disaster.[28]

In an effort to promote newscasters and make them seem more "real," they were promoted as, and became, celebrities. When Rose Ann Scamardella gave birth to a child, she received "thousands of cards, sweaters and booties . . . and every year, viewers remember her [daughter's] birthday."[29]

But even those celebrities were becoming cynical. "They've called the "Eyewitness News' format revolutionary," said WABC-TV's Tolliver, "but it is a pitiful revolution for television if all they could do was make people seem real. I would like to be able to switch the TV dial to different stations and not see identical coverage of the news, sports, politics, weather. That would be a real breakthrough."[30] Or, as Rivera told Powers: "I mean, the television news bosses see to it that their personalities become stars. *Stars* in direct proportion with their popularity."[31]

Everything WABC-TV did would soon find its way to Detroit. The entire front anchor team at WABC-TV dressed in blue blazers. Before long the entire anchor team at WXYZ-TV went on the air with blue blazers. And it worked. By 1972 WXYZ-TV was the number one news station in town.

The money made by WXYZ-TV and other ABC stations proved irresistible to most in the television business. If ABC made money turning news into a show, others would do the same. As Les Brown of the *New York Times* wrote: "Stations in practically every market in the country are working at changing the appearance; the length; the style and the journalistic standards of their newscasts to improve their ratings—and, as a result, their profits."[32]

In May 1972 WNBC introduced a new newscast with all of the touches and noise of a television show. The program began with music from the film *Shaft.* The on-camera "set" was conceived by the designer who had constructed the *Jesus Christ Superstar* set on Broadway. John O'Connor wrote that it resembled "a mini-amphitheatre . . . the image, unfortunately is that of an operating room, suggesting that just below the two anchormen, off-camera, rests a cadaver ready for dissecting."[33] What this meant was that "television news" was concentrating more on "television" and less on "news." When the miniamphitheatre set failed, the station introduced something even bigger and bolder. Called *NewsCenter4*, it featured yet another news set and new group of anchors, including Los Angeles newsman Tom Snyder, who had most recently hosted NBC-TV's *Tomorrow* program.

Other Detroit stations saw WXYZ-TV's success and tried, in their fashion, to enter the "personality" news business. With its ratings beginning to plummet, WWJ-TV caught the show business bug and hired anchorman Dean Miller in 1973. Miller's résumé was long on entertainment, short on news experience. He had hosted a morning show, *There's One in Every Family*, in the early 1950s, and played Matt Henshaw on CBS's *December Bride* between 1954 and 1959. Miller used his Hollywood money to buy a few radio stations and a weekly newspaper in Ohio. He decided to get into anchoring and established himself as a newsman in Miami, where WWJ-TV executives found him. In other words, he was not a journalist, but he could play one on television. His hiring created resentment in the WWJ-TV newsroom.[34] Each of WWJ-TV's past anchors had had news experience. Miller had little journalism in his background.

It was here that WWJ-TV threw the television news equivalent of the Hail Mary pass. It hired the first woman anchor in the history of Detroit television. Betty Carrier was a Birmingham native who first thought about television as a Wayne State University student. "I was told by my counselor at the time that that was pointless, because there weren't any women at that time in broadcasting to speak of," she later recalled. Carrier plunged ahead, got her degree, started out at Pontiac's WPON-AM, and later worked as the radio and television press representative for the United Foundation. She was hired in late 1969 by WWJ-TV, which was looking specifically for a woman reporter. "They didn't know what to do with me," she remembered. "I was the only other woman in the Channel 4 newsroom at that time, other than the administrative assistant. . . . They got me, but they weren't sure exactly where to put me, how to plot out stories for me. Should I be a street reporter? Should I be just an anchor?" She recalled that everybody at the station was helpful to her.[35]

In 1973, only four years after Carrier reported her first television story, WWJ-TV's managers decided to take a chance with Carrier at the anchor desk during the station's most important newscasts. The women's liberation movement was in full force, and some thought putting a woman in a key role at 7:00 p.m. and 11:00 p.m. would help the station's ratings. She worked with the team of Dean Miller, Sonny Eliot, and Jim Forney. All were supportive. Her recollection of the audience reaction:

> Audiences were not in tune with having a woman [at the anchor desk]. It all seems so odd to talk about it now, because it's so common. . . . The phone calls I used to get were really something else, particularly from the women. "I don't like the way she does her hair. I don't like the clothes she's wearing." . . . It was always comments about my personal look, rather than the content. It kind of got in the way, it really did. It was a hard bridge to cross to make people listen to what you were saying, rather than what you were wearing or how your hair was done. I don't mean like everybody was that way. But there were a lot of critical comments based on my looks. . . . Women were not sure how to accept all of this, apparently.[36]

The experiment did not work. Carrier got the job in April, but moved back to the lower-profile newscasts by the end of the year. *Detroit Free Press* TV writer Bettelou Peterson told readers, "The ladies have to remember that equal chance means equal hazard, too. . . . There is too much money and prestige involved in the acceptance of the local newscasts to play it altogether noble."[37] In late 1974, she left the station to have a son, John, who was born January 2, 1975.

WWJ-TV, the key video component of the Evening News Association information juggernaut, was beginning to fade. Local television's new era demanded personalities. WWJ-TV had little personality to offer, or at least not the kind of personality Detroit viewers enjoyed.

The ratings within several months of the riot told the story (see appendix, table 32). WWJ-TV's hegemony, precarious immediately after the 1967 riots, ceased entirely. Viewers were becoming accustomed to more than just "the news." They were being entertained. If they cared not a whit for news, they could still tune in for drama, for excitement, for Bill Bonds and his fabulous arching eyebrows. How would WWJ-TV react?

The company reacted by selling a political message. Form may have become increasingly important elsewhere, but not to the officials at WWJ-TV. They had a message. The fact that their message would make the station look disagreeable to many Detroit television viewers would apparently not matter—at least not in the short run. In the long run, however, that miscalculation would become extremely expensive.

6. WWJ-TV'S SWING TO THE RIGHT

WWJ-TV offered a political point of view. The Evening News Association (ENA), in addition to facing a changing climate in the broadcast industry, also faced Detroit's volatile political climate during the late 1960s and early 1970s. The company reacted conservatively via the pages of the *Detroit News* and WWJ-TV's airwaves. While WXYZ-TV experimented with personality-driven news, and WJBK-TV tried inventive journalistic and visual methods to stay competitive, WWJ-TV took on a conservative, curmudgeonly image. The image did not appear as a result of any one event. It surfaced as a result of hiring and firing choices, programming decisions, editorial judgment at the *Detroit News*, and even architectural selections. WWJ-TV's previous success in the 1950s and 1960s fogged the vision of station officials. This chapter examines each of these factors, which culminated in a ratings slide from first place in news during the 1950s and 1960s to last place by the mid-1970s.

A company's headquarters is considered a company's face. Not long after the 1967 riot, the Evening News Association chose to hide its face, bricking up its downtown Detroit headquarters and turning the building into what the *New York Times* called a "fortress."[1] Before the architectural revamping, the *Detroit News* building, which also served as headquarters for the ENA, featured a large set of windows that permitted pedestrians to view the hulking, spinning presses from the street. Those windows were replaced by brick, a decision made immediately after the 1967 riot but not executed until late 1968 because of a nine-month newspaper strike that closed the paper in 1967–68. "[Traveling around the city], anyone can see a number of windows broken, mostly in retail establishments," said Peter B. Clark, chairman of the Evening News Association and publisher of the *Detroit News*. The company also instituted new security measures that forced employees and visitors to show identification at a checkpoint in the WWJ-TV and *News* lobbies. "We thought it would be a better idea to know who was coming into the newspaper building," Clark added.[2] The newspaper employees did not think so. One told the *New York Times* anonymously, "There are more important things to do than to brick up windows and wear ID cards."[3]

The security moves could have been strictly interpreted by the public as having to do only with the ENA and *Detroit News*, although WWJ-TV employees were also forced to show ID badges at the station headquarters. However, WWJ-TV and the *News* were intertwined in the Detroit public consciousness. WWJ-TV, WWJ-AM, and WWJ-FM each identified itself on air as "WWJ, the Detroit News." WWJ-AM had done so since 1920, WWJ-TV since 1947, and WWJ-FM since 1941. *Detroit News* reporters delivered the news on WWJ-TV during a twenty-nine day strike in 1962.[4] As mentioned, WWJ-TV's studios were directly across the street from the *News* building. There were other connections. The University of Michigan band had announced that it would stage an antiwar demonstration on the football field in Ann Arbor during a University of Michigan–Indiana University football game in 1971.[5] WWJ-AM radio officials were ordered by ENA officials to pull their microphones from the field and cover other stories from the studio, according to Louis Prato, a WWJ-TV/WWJ-AM news director during the period.[6]

All the while, ENA and WWJ-TV officials tried to make it appear to the Federal Communications Commission as if the two organizations were separate. For example, WWJ-TV did not run on-air editorials until 1971. According to DeGroot: "Peter Clark and I had discussed the desirability of editorializing several times, but the question of who would determine WWJ Stations' editorial policy would have to be resolved. To link us with the *Detroit News* policy would, in my opinion, be disastrous in the eyes of the FCC and might seem to indicate to the general public that we were *Detroit News* dominated when we were, in all other respects, autonomous."[7] Whether or not the station and newspaper were truly separate was a subject that could be debated. But there was a connection. The connection had been a selling point among viewers in the 1950s and early 1960s. However, the *News* became a somewhat divisive topic after the 1967 riots, particularly when it came to race. In 1968 the newspaper began running a daily crime blotter on page 2 that identified suspects by race. Typical of the newspaper's Crime in Detroit column:

The assailant was described as a Negro, about 27, 5 feet 8, 170 pounds, wearing a light gray shirt and dark pants. . . . Three young men, one armed with a revolver, held up Our Enterprises, 3914 Joy, near McQuade, on the near west side, at 5 p.m. yesterday. One was a Negro, 17, 5 feet 5, thin and wearing a black narrow brim hat and a rust-colored suit. The second was a Negro, 17, 5 feet 6, thin and dressed in a white shirt and khaki pants. . . . A *Detroit News* carrier boy, Michael Lawrence, 12, was robbed by two boys at 3:50 p.m. yesterday as he delivered newspapers on Selden near Second. One was 5 feet 5, slim, wearing dirty white pants. The other was 5 feet 4 and wore a green shirt and black pants torn at the knees. Both are Negroes.[8]

The practice triggered a boycott in the city's African American community. The newspaper was unapologetic. As the newspaper's editors wrote:

Yes we do identify the race of the suspect. In doing so, we follow what we believe to be a realistic and completely nonracist policy which has been in effect on this paper much longer than charges of racism have been popular. We identify race only when we have some other descriptive detail and the suspected criminal is still be sought. . . . True we have aroused criticism. Now when will we arouse the inner city to forget fear, reject apathy and actively join the effort to catch criminals and help to stop crime in Detroit?"[9]

Such editorials annoyed many in Detroit. And those who were annoyed with the *News* could not help but connect the *News* with WWJ-TV, fairly or not.

Researcher Philip McHugh picked up WWJ-TV's problem in surveys for WJBK-TV. He told WJBK-TV officials in 1968:

Detroiters—still recovering from last summer and fearing a possible reoccurrence this year—are acutely sensitive to all issues of civil rights and in some way, Channel 4's presentations have not been satisfactory in this regard. It is not clear from the data exactly how WWJ-TV is not satisfying, but the criticism is there, and more often than not it revolves around civil rights issues, being criticized by both Negroes and whites for giving the "wrong slant" (depending on the individual viewer's stand), for not being "complete enough," and not giving "the full story."[10]

The station was to pay heavily in terms of viewers. Arbitron, the television survey company, measured viewing habits among metropolitan

Detroit's African American households in November 1976. The survey showed that Detroit's African American community had all but abandoned WWJ-TV. Table 33 (see appendix) shows WWJ-TV's 11:00 p.m. news rating and share. (A rating is the newscast's percentage of viewership among all television households in Detroit's black community. Share is the percentage of viewers watching television during the 11–11:30 p.m. time period.) As can be seen, WJBK-TV's share of viewing among black households was triple that of WWJ-TV, while WXYZ-TV held a two-to-one advantage.

The company sent out other signals on the topic of the brewing social turmoil of the 1960s and early 1970s. Convinced that NBC News displayed a left-wing bias in its coverage of the Vietnam War and other issues, senior station officials hired a conservative commentator to critique NBC News' coverage—a predecessor of the present-day Fox News Channel or Rush Limbaugh. Dr. Fred E. Dohrs, a Wayne State University geography professor, delivered a three-minute "rebuttal" following the *NBC Nightly News* between January 1972 and October 1975. The determination to hire a conservative commentator was born in the offices of Peter B. Clark, chairman of the board of the Evening News Association since 1963. DeGroot explained,

> It was particularly distressing to me to me that virtually every network reporter colored his story by ending with a "zinger," so that even when a story appeared balanced in content, the tag-line converted it to an editorial that emphasized the extremely liberal viewpoint of the reporter or made a damaging assertion against "establishment," or took aim at any stabilizing status quo. It appeared to us that network newsmen were trying to alter the world into the image they sought whether or not that image was justified.[11]

DeGroot supplied no specifics in his autobiography, but Clark ordered station technicians to tape the *NBC Nightly News.* In addition, both Clark and DeGroot ordered that producers use no NBC News footage in the station's 11:00 p.m. newscasts.[12] A meeting was arranged between NBC chairman Julian Goodman and Detroiters Clark, DeGroot, and one other Evening News Association official. Goodman heard Clark's complaints but defended his journalists. Complaints by NBC affiliates about the network's news department were not unusual during the Vietnam War era. After

Vice President Spiro T. Agnew made his famous Des Moines speech on November 13, 1969, attacking network executives and commentators as elitist, NBC News president Reuven Frank wrote, "[P]roprietors of the affiliated stations publicly declared support for the network news division, but they told reporters from behind their hands that there was a lot in what Agnew said." Later, NBC affiliates approved a resolution that the news division was "biased, unbalanced and unfair" by a margin of 60 percent to 40 percent. Frank termed the vote "a stunning result, especially given the almost automatic loyalty most affiliates still displayed for their networks. I assume at least half of those who voted against the resolution agreed with it but were reluctant to be recorded as disloyal."[13]

WWJ-TV officials had no such reluctance. As DeGroot later wrote, the ENA decided on a "'zinger' of our own" and hired Dohrs to critique NBC News' presentation.[14] His segment was called *Newswatch*, and it anticipated a point of view later popularized by conservative radio entertainer Rush Limbaugh. WWJ-TV press releases discussing Dohrs's work carried the footnote "'Newswatch' is telecast weekly as a means of counterbalancing subjective reporting from national and international sources."[15]

Dohrs, who had earned a PhD in geography from Northwestern University in 1950, later traveled extensively in Yugoslavia, Czechoslovakia, Poland, eastern Germany, and Hungary. He also shuffled in and out of government work during the 1950s and 1960s. At the height of the cold war, Dohrs served as a visiting professor of political geography at the government's Naval War College (1958–59), as a visiting lecturer on Eastern Europe at the U.S. State Department's Foreign Service Institute (1960), and as director of policy and research on Communist areas for Radio Free Europe (1960), an organization covertly aligned with the CIA.[16] Dohrs was working as chairman of Wayne State University's geography department at the time of his hiring at WWJ-TV, and continued in the post while working as a television commentator.

In his *Newswatch* segments, Dohrs would usually examine an NBC News story of the previous day or two and comment on the story and/or the reporter's alleged liberal bias. For example, Dohrs delivered a commentary on October 15, 1975, taking issue with an NBC News report on a natural-gas shortage. An NBC newsman had reported simply, "Supplies will fall short of the anticipated demand. . . . That means factories which cannot use other fuels will have to shut down and lay off their workers. And if it's a cold winter, the layoffs could be widespread."[17]

The report may seem a simple statement of fact. But Dohrs, in one of his final *Newswatch* commentaries, did not see it that way. He claimed:

NBC News apparently wanted to leave the impression that the U.S. has exhausted its supplies of natural gas. The facts are just the opposite. In recent years, production of natural gas in the United States hasn't grown as fast as demand—not because of any shortage of gas reserves, but because the Federal Power Commission, which controls prices on all natural gas entering interstate commerce, has kept gas prices artificially low. . . . It must be made clear—because NBC News did not—that the consequences of a natural gas shortage, and the shortage itself, result from excessive government regulation. And, once again, price controls have resulted in harming those consumers such regulations were supposed to help.[18]

The commentaries were not taken seriously in the newsrooms. "I would turn the set off when he came on. They were that deadly," joked Louis Prato.[19] Had Clark, DeGroot, or any of their colleagues known about Prato's reaction, he could have been fired. ENA officials were unusually proud of Dohrs's work. DeGroot, upon the invitation of U.S. senator Robert Griffin (R-MI), took a selection of Dohrs's tapes to Washington, DC, for a showing among congressmen. Another showing was arranged at the White House. Wrote DeGroot, "We had anticipated President Nixon joining us to see the tapes, but we were advised that vital matters of State kept him from doing so. We discovered sometime later that our visit coincided with the date Mr. Nixon first encountered some of the realities of the Watergate break in."[20]

Unbeknownst to television viewers, Dohr had another employer: the Central Intelligence Agency. Channel 4's management found out after a letter from the White House appeared one day in Dohrs's mailbox. Dohrs was on vacation, so a mailroom clerk brought it to the attention of news chief Jim Clark. Clark opened the envelope and found an invitation to a dinner with President Richard Nixon. Clark called around, and found Dohrs at CIA headquarters in Langley, Virginia. Dohrs's reaction: "You've blown my cover."[21]

Dohrs's appearances were a violation of journalistic ethnics, although not because of his CIA work. Detroit television viewers were never informed of Dohrs's CIA employment, necessary information in judging his credibility.

There were other missteps. WWJ-TV began airing commentaries by S. L. A. Marshall, a military historian who had joined the *News* in 1920. As the Vietnam War became more prominent in the news, Channel 4's management allowed Marshall airtime for commentary. The reaction was overwhelmingly negative. McHugh and Hoffman researchers, who were working for Channel 2, showed tapes of Marshall's editorials to a focus group. "The reaction of our panelists to this gentlemen and his commentaries was unfavorable, to say the least," wrote the researchers in a memo. "While for the most part they appeared to agree with the spirit of his commentaries, they were put on edge by his manner of delivery and his appearance. In particular they disliked his apparently belligerent attitude and his harsh unpleasant voice and looks." The researchers quoted panelists as saying: "S. L. A. Marshall gives me a royal pain" (Male, Middle Class)." "It's like most of these retired generals and majors. They sit down and blither out their opinions (Male, Middle Class)."[22] Researcher Peter S. Hoffman, who conducted a market study for WJBK-TV, wrote in 1974 that local television viewers saw WWJ-TV as "ultra-conservative, behind the times."[23]

Commentaries by Dohrs and Marshall were overshadowed by the controversial dismissal of WWJ-TV sportscaster Al Ackerman in 1972. Ackerman was Detroit's most popular, innovative, and debated-about sportscasters during the 1960s and early 1970s. Ackerman broke the mold of the typical Detroit sportscaster, lacing the scores with his own brand of acerbic commentary. For instance, Ackerman was mightily offended by the fact that taxpayers in blue-collar Pontiac paid to build the Pontiac Silverdome for the Detroit Lions—owned by William Clay Ford, one of the world's richest men. Ackerman would refer to the Silverdome as the "Teflondome." Ackerman looked at sports reporting as a serious form of journalism, not the "toy department" that some considered it to be.

Ackerman hit the front pages after a commentary about the 1972 Olympic games. Two African American athletes declined to stand while receiving their awards. The symbolic gesture sparked irate comment around the country. Ackerman had a different take. He felt there was something else to be outraged about—the murder of eleven Israeli athletes and coaches by a group of terrorists. "Under the circumstances I can't feel the same sense of outrage as some of our viewers with the murder of eleven Olympians still fresh in my mind." Ackerman was summoned to DeGroot's office and fired. The *Detroit Free Press* story, which ran on page 1 of Sunday's newspaper and reported hundreds of telephone calls to its "Soundoff" telephone lines, said that the tape of the comment was not available, and "Ackerman's script was reportedly missing from its normal place."[24] The *Detroit News* did not run an account of Ackerman's dismissal.

DeGroot's own account of the incident, published in an autobiography that was written for family and friends, displayed inconsistencies. It is worth examining DeGroot's account as a road map to his thinking, and that of other WWJ-TV and Evening News officials, during the era.

Commenting on sports events was one thing; editorializing on administrative and political affairs was another. When two Olympic athletes ostentatiously ignored the American flag and the playing of the national anthem, Al chose to comment that that did not disturb him; he was much more concerned about the murder of eleven Olympians which had occurred earlier in the sessions. Had he, perhaps, commented on the murder alone, there might have been no repercussions. But a seeming lack of concern over disdain of the flag and anthem angered a hoard of viewers who telephoned persistently afterward. . . . I ordered that his employment with us be terminated at once. Most unhappily, he left that day. That it was the eve of a Jewish high holiday had not occurred to me, although I was later accused of having chosen that hallowed time vindictively."[25]

DeGroot admitted later that he did not foresee viewer reaction, which was mainly favorable to Ackerman. He was "pestered" by viewers for firing Ackerman, a curious choice of words for a man who operated a station on behalf of the "public interest and convenience."[26] A close examination of DeGroot's account would reasonably yield the conclusion that DeGroot was more upset by Ackerman's stance ("seeming lack of concern over disdain of the flag and anthem") than Ackerman's editorializing. Ackerman, in fact, had become famous in Detroit for his constant editorializing. He later joined WXYZ-TV, where he became successful, before returning to WDIV-TV—the call letters of his old station after the ENA sold the broadcast concern to the *Washington Post* Company.

But the Ackerman firing was only the most visible sign of the turmoil that characterized WWJ-TV. Local television in Detroit and other cities experimented with personalities, consultants, and investigative reporting. But WWJ-TV would have none of that. David Kelly, a veteran Pittsburgh and Washington, DC, newsman, was brought in by WWJ-TV in 1970 to replace Clark, who had been running WWJ-TV's newsroom since 1953. Kelly and his newly hired assistant, Louis Prato, were disturbed at what they found. According to Prato, Kelly had been hired to revamp the station's newscasts. But when Kelly did offer suggestions, he was ignored. Prato explained:

> The town was pissed off at the *Detroit News.* They [WWJ-TV executives] weren't staying abreast of it [changes in television]. Kelly was brought in to change things. One of the reasons he left was they wouldn't listen to him. . . . They thought they knew what the answers were under Peter B. Clark because they had done all of this before. They had been uno supremo. Nobody got fired there. Everybody retired, got kicked upstairs. There was so much deadwood around there.[27]

Two of the newsmen who were burying WWJ-TV, ironically, were former WWJ-TV employees. One was William Fyffe, now WXYZ-TV's news director. The other was reporter Ven Marshall, who had been dismissed by WWJ-TV but immediately hired by WXYZ-TV. "They were doing investigative reporting, they were commanding the story while we were sitting back. We couldn't make any headway. And I got blamed for it," complained Prato.[28]

One of the reasons WWJ-TV would not do investigative reporting was fear of offending advertisers. Prato, with the blessing of general manager DeGroot, had assigned a reporter to take a mechanically perfect automobile to various auto repair shops to find how they would diagnose it. Many of the shops came up with phony repair estimates, ranging into the hundreds of dollars. When it came time to air the broadcast, DeGroot shut Prato down. What follows is Prato's account of his conversation with DeGroot:

I said, "OK, Don, I'm ready to show you the working print on the car investigation."

DeGroot: What car investigation?

Prato: The one you approved.

DeGroot: We're not going to air it.

Prato: You've got to at least look at it.

DeGroot: We're not going to air it.[29]

An angry Prato visited DeGroot thirty minutes later to make another plea. "Don, we've spent a lot of time on this. If we don't air this story, my credibility is going to be bad," he argued. Prato talked about newsroom morale. DeGroot would not relent, explaining, "They [the car dealers] will kill their advertising."[30] Shortly thereafter Prato was fired.

There was another reason for poor newsroom morale at WWJ-TV. Ratings during the mid-1970s were getting worse. Arbitron's measurement of metropolitan Detroit's viewing habits at 11:00 p.m. are shown in table 34 (see appendix). The numbers include each station's rating (the percentage of television sets in metropolitan Detroit) and share (the percentage of television sets in use during a given time period). As can be seen, the station's ratings and share dropped each year between 1974 and 1977 before recovering slightly in 1978. During two of those years, 1976 and 1977, WWJ-TV's ratings were half of WXYZ-TV, the ratings leader during those years.

Even more telling was the tune-out factor. No station during the 1970s saw a heavier defection from the last half hour of network programming between the 10:30 and 11:00 p.m. network prime-time hour and the 11:00 p.m. local news hour. Each station suffered the vicissitudes of its network's performance between 10:30 and 11:00 p.m. If a network delivered a large audience at 10:30 p.m. with popular entertainment programming, chances were that some considerable portion of the audience would remain at 11:00. But WWJ-TV's ratings suffered no matter what NBC-TV aired during the period. Table 35 (see appendix) shows the stations' average rating between 10:30 and 11:00 p.m. each February between 1974 and 1978, and each station's average rating between 11:00 and 11:30 p.m. WWJ-TV routinely saw at least one-third of its audience melt away at 11:00 p.m. Other stations suffered the same problem, but not in that magnitude. In each year between 1974 and 1978 it led the pack in audience defection at 11:00 p.m. The station tried numerous fixes. It shuffled three lead male anchors into the station's most visible news job between 1974 and 1978. By way of comparison, only two men had held the job between 1955 and 1973. It shuffled news directors in and out, with four people holding the job in the 1970s. One person had held the job between 1953 and 1970. While WXYZ-TV had seemingly mastered the new world of local television journalism, WWJ-TV had not.

One can interpret WWJ-TV's failure in two ways. One could say that the station management's political point of view was alien to a large number of viewers. Or one could argue that the station fell behind in the fast-moving world of local television news. Either way, the Evening News Association's ownership of WWJ-TV was about to come to an end.

First radio appearance, January 31, 1922, over WWJ during vaudeville engagement at Temple Theater. The Detroit News reported " Babe Ruth bats .999 by radio-phone".

BABE RUTH

New York Yankee slugger Babe Ruth at WWJ, January 31, 1922.

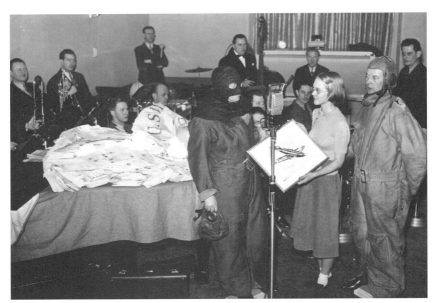

The Black Ace, a locally written serial, which aired on WWJ-AM.

Broadway playwright/composer George M. Cohan (*center*), interviewed on WWJ-AM by George Stark (*left*) in 1936.

WWJ-AM's control room, located in the *Detroit News* garage, 1936.

The Detroit News Orchestra, a frequent presence on WWJ-AM, circa 1926.

The first complete announcer's panel, built by Edwin G. Boyes, 1926.

WWJ-AM—a radio station with its own auditorium and orchestra.

WWJ executive Harry Bannister, who rose from salesman to general manager during his two decades at the station. The photograph was shot in 1941. He joined NBC in 1952 as a vice president in charge of station relations.

The WWJ display at the Michigan State Fair, 1923.

Sonny Eliot, starring in the play *Suppressed Desires*, 1960.

WWJ-AM's studios, 1922. The drapes are there for acoustic effect.

The WWJ-TV test pattern.

WWJ-TV live broadcast, year unknown.

Crowds gather to hear play-by-play accounts of the World Series, as broadcast on WWJ-AM.

Detroit News columnist H. C. L. Jackson reads into the camera, 1946. Reprinted by permission of the *Detroit News*.

Crowds watching Detroit's first television broadcast, 1946, at the city's Convention Hall. Reprinted by permission of the *Detroit News*.

Anchorman Ken Manuel reporting election returns, 1948. Reprinted by permission of the *Detroit News.*

The *Detroit News'* William E. Scripps behind the company airplane—among the first in metropolitan Detroit. Reprinted by permission of the *Detroit News.*

WWJ-TV's Paul Williams (*left*) with University of Michigan's Wally Weber broadcasting a University of Michigan vs. Michigan State University game, 1948. Reprinted by permission of the *Detroit News*.

Anchorman Jac Le Goff adjusts his microphone on the Channel 7 set, 1983. Reprinted by permission of the *Detroit News*.

Jac Le Goff in 1968, at the height of his popularity at Channel 2.
Reprinted by permission of the *Detroit News.*

WWJ-AM celebrates twenty-five years on the air, 1945. *From left to right*: Thomas Clark (who helped put WWJ on the air); *Detroit News* executive William E. Scripps; his son, William J. Scripps; and actor Walter Hampden—one of the stars of *Sabrina* and *All about Eve*. Reprinted by permission of the *Detroit News*.

Lou Gordon, angry and playing to the crowds, speaks out against a utility rate hike, 1976. Reprinted by permission of the *Detroit News*.

George Pierrot surveys the globe, circa 1972. Reprinted by permission of the *Detroit News*.

Lou Gordon shakes hands with a somber George Wallace, 1968. Gordon questioned Wallace's sanity. Reprinted by permission of the *Detroit News*.

Ven Marshall at the Channel 4 election desk, 1966. Incumbent governor George Romney beat Democrat Zolton Ferency that year. Reprinted by permission of the *Detroit News*.

A crowd watching television in the Kern's Department Store window, downtown Detroit, 1947. Reprinted by permission of the *Detroit News*.

WWJ-TV sportscaster Paul Williams in the announcer's booth at a Detroit Red Wings hockey game, 1949. Reprinted by permission of the *Detroit News*.

Channel 50's Lou Gordon. Reprinted by permission of the *Detroit News.*

Jac Le Goff at the Channel 7 anchor desk, 1983. Reprinted by permission of the *Detroit News.*

Mr. and Mrs. Wally Kisp, with *The Coffee Club* host Dave Zimmerman looking on. This is said to be the first kiss on Detroit television, October 1946. Reprinted by permission of the *Detroit News.*

The first television broadcast, at Detroit's Convention Hall, October 1946. Reprinted by permission of the *Detroit News.*

William E. Scripps, who got the *Detroit News* into the broadcasting business, in front of the camera; behind it is his son, William J. Scripps. Reprinted by permission of the *Detroit News.*

Detroit television at work. Reprinted by permission of the *Detroit News.*

Detroit mayor Edward Jeffries Jr. checks out the equipment in 1946. Next to him is William J. Scripps, a member of the family that owned the *Detroit News.* Reprinted by permission of the *Detroit News.*

A crowd watches the first Detroit television broadcast, October 1946. Reprinted by permission of the *Detroit News.*

Outdoorsman Mort Neff setting up a magnetic recording device in the snow, circa 1952. Reprinted by permission of the *Detroit News*.

7. TURBULENCE ON THE AIR

A s of early 1978, the players in Detroit television journalism had remained the same for thirty years. But a new station owner arrived in Detroit in 1978, an owner with different ideas about how to attract an audience. Those ideas were grounded more in traditional journalism than in the Happy Talk setting. As this chapter will show, the old approach paid off—but only after those ideas were sold in a different way. Meanwhile, WJBK-TV began sinking after WXYZ-TV literally bought many of the station's best-known news personnel.

The sale of WWJ-TV involved court decisions and high-level dealings between the scions of two great newspaper families. Even as WWJ-TV coped with the new television environment, a case was wending its way through the federal court system that would eventually trigger new ownership of the station. The Federal Communications Commission announced in 1970 that it would examine the effects of television ownership by newspaper companies. After study, the FCC stated that it would not change existing cross-ownership rules. The National Citizens Committee for Broadcasting, a consumer advocate group, filed suit challenging the decision. The U.S. Court of Appeals in Washington, DC, agreed with the group, and on March 1, 1977, invalidated the FCC's rule permitting newspaper publishers to own broadcast concerns in the same market in which they published.[1] The ruling, if it stood, would have caused publishers to divest themselves of their television stations.

Publishers began seeking ways to avoid potential divestitures. "Although second-guessing the Supreme Court can be a tricky business, this case is causing a flurry of backstage activity among publishers and broadcasters who will be forced to divest some of their properties if the Court upholds the appeal," wrote Deirdre Carmody, a veteran *New York Times* correspondent.[2] The *Washington Post*'s Katherine Graham and the ENA's Peter B. Clark, who held just such backstage meetings, announced in December 1977 that the two media conglomerates would swap their respective television stations. The *Post*'s WTOP-TV would go to the ENA, along with $2 million. The *Post* would get WWJ-TV. Ironically, the U.S. Supreme Court, in June 1978, reversed the U.S. Court of Appeals. Although newspapers could no longer buy broadcast properties in their hometowns, the old newspapers/broadcast combinations would be grandfathered in. The *New York Times* analysis of the Supreme Court decision reported government statistics that would have seemed to make the case academic. "According to FCC figures, the share of television channels controlled by newspapers has been dropping steadily from forty percent in 1950 to 14 percent in 1969 to 10 percent in 1975."[3] Academic or not, the *Post* took control of WWJ-TV in June 1978 and renamed it WDIV-TV.[4] The D stood for Detroit, the IV for the Roman numeral 4.

News director Jim Snyder was the first Post-Newsweek executive to take power after Post-Newsweek Stations obtained WWJ-TV. Snyder had been a Washington producer for CBS News before joining Post-Newsweek, which owns the *Washington Post* and *Newsweek* magazine, in 1968. While there, he hired Max Robinson, who went on to become an ABC News anchorman. His plans for WDIV-TV would not take root until the early 1980s, a thoughtful approach totally alien to the ambulance-chasing culture of those days. He placed a high premium on honesty and ethics.

"To Snyder, it was a news director's job to know the community he worked in and what kind of newscast to put together," recalled Harrison S. Wyman in an appreciation of Snyder's work after Snyder's death in 2001. "Snyder thought it was important that television news report stories you may not like to hear but needed to know."[5] According to Terry Oprea, who worked for Snyder: "If there ever was a real-life Lou Grant, this was the guy. . . . He really loathed the idea of covering murder for the sake of murder. He believed that if you were going to cover something like that, you had to have a reason. He wanted us to cover the culture, the fabric, the texture of the community."[6]

Even as Snyder was remaking the news department, Post-Newsweek forced out many of WWJ-TV's older personalities. Nobody was safe. George Pierrot, who had been on Detroit television since 1948, retired. *Oopsy! the Clown*, an old-line Detroit children's show, was taken off the air. So was *Bowling for Dollars*, a weekday program taped at an Allen Park bowling alley. Bob Allison, the show's host, was still bitter about the cancellation years later. "I bowled for years with the guys from the Detroit Athletic Club [one of Detroit's best clubs], and I never saw any of them with a lunch bucket or a blue collar. Most of them could've bought and sold Channel 4 [the station that cancelled *Bowling for Dollars*] if they felt like it."[7]

Snyder's first high-profile hire was anchorman Mort Crim. Crim, the son of an Indiana preacher and a graduate of Northwestern University's Medill School of Journalism, broke into broadcast journalism with ABC Radio, where he covered space flights during the 1960s. He moved to television in the early 1970s in Louisville, Kentucky, then joined Philadelphia's KYW-TV. Crim and anchorwoman Jessica Savitch had been successful there. After Savitch left for NBC News, Crim joined Chicago's WBBM-TV, a CBS-owned station. His experience in Chicago was an unhappy one. Snyder convinced Crim that WDIV-TV would be a great challenge for a newsman in midcareer. Crim was held in high esteem throughout the country. As Crim arrived in Detroit, ABC News president Roone Arledge's searched for a new ABC anchorman. Arledge seriously considered pairing Crim with Peter Jennings before settling on Max Robinson.[8]

The new team did not realize the kind of challenge it would be. "The station was a mess," recalled producer Oprea. "They had changed strategies about every ten minutes during the 1970s, so the viewers never knew what to expect." Crim was met with suspicion. "He was an 'outsider,'" explained Oprea.[9]

Katherine Graham, chairman of the Washington Post Company, was particularly distressed by the company's troubles in Detroit. As she related in her autobiography,

> The situation in Detroit was worse than my worst fears. We had traded a top-flight station in a dynamic market for a mediocre station in a market that was mired in a recession. On top of that, the station was an NBC affiliate, and NBC at the time was a network in trouble. We had our usual new-in-the-market problems: we wanted to run a better station, but resistance to change was endemic, and Detroiters were used to having their news delivered in a certain way, no matter how bad it may have been. Again, as in Trenton [where Post-Newsweek owned a television station] we were painted as the out-of-towners. Any time we made a mistake or tried something new, critics at the other stations or the newspapers leapt on us. It was so bad that Jim Snyder had a serious heart attack and had to leave. I suffered acutely at having decided to make the trade, particularly after the Supreme Court handed down

its decision, grandfathering those companies who already had stations in cross-ownership towns. Little by little, the Detroit station improved and became very successful, but that didn't happen before I spent an inordinate amount of time blaming myself.[10]

To get around the "outsider" image, WDIV-TV officials created a public affairs show that would showcase Crim to the Detroit audience in a positive way. "Mort had gotten here but nobody knew who he was, other than that he had a booming voice. We needed to show him walking around, talking to an audience," said Harvey Ovshinsky, one of the show's creators. The show's producers assembled a group of five panelists, who argued about the issues of the day before a live audience. Crim served as the moderator/emcee/referee. Ovshinsky explained the show to *Detroit Free Press* TV critic Mike Duffy as "What's My Line panel Meets the Press in front of a Donahue audience." Duffy liked what he saw, toasting the show as "informative and entertaining."[11]

The quintet included Mike Sessa, a tax cutter from Macomb County; Larry Simmons, of the Detroit Urban League; Diane Trombley, a nurse who was active in the state's pro-life movement; Joan Israel, a social worker and feminist therapist; and Janice Burnett, who worked in the mental health field. The discussions were sometimes noisy but usually shed more light than heat—unlike a later generation of news talk shows, where the opposite was true. Crim was highlighted as a guy who could relate well across class and race lines.

Mike Sessa was later elected to a post on the Macomb County Board of Commissioners. But the show was only part of the strategy. The other part involved building a strong journalistic team around Crim. WDIV-TV hired on-air reporters from local radio stations, from the *Detroit News*, and from NBC News. While on-air presence was important, Snyder placed a higher premium on journalistic skill than on previous local television experience. Few Detroit television stations had recently hired print reporters. Snyder hired two. Among the new team of journalists was Robert Pisor, whose résumé included stints as a political writer at the *Detroit News*, as editor of *Detroit Monthly* magazine, and as a press secretary to Detroit mayor Coleman A. Young. Pisor also wrote a book, *The End of the Line: The Siege of Khe Sanh*, which appraised one of the Vietnam War's most significant battles.[12]

Pisor first signed on at WDIV-TV as the station's media critic, in which position he delivered trenchant appraisals of the *Detroit News* and *Detroit Free Press.* He soon became the station's political reporter and weekend anchorman.

The station also hired a business journalist. She was Jennifer Moore, a female addition to a formerly all-male preserve. An Ohio native, Moore began her Detroit journalism career at WJR-AM in 1975. She quickly made her mark in Detroit as a youthful, energetic reporter who had a great feeling for journalism's oldest and best qualities. "She was younger than the other WJR staffers, but she approached news in the classic WJR way. . . . They [some of the younger reporters] didn't have that appreciation for accuracy, of the trust the public placed in the better news organizations. But she did. That made her stand out," recalled radio newsman Dick Haefner, who was a WWJ-AM reporter in the 1970s and later became WJR's news director. "She had the classic qualities and principles of the best reporters. She appreciated business news and understood it for what it was—general news about money. I thought her business reporting shined."[13]

Finally, Snyder hired reporter/anchor Emery King from NBC News. King had been a reporter at CBS-owned WBBM-TV and at NBC News. He joined WDIV-TV for two reasons. One was personal. He had decided he did not want to spend his life on airplanes, which is the lot of a television network reporter. He had seen the rise of NBC News' Bryant Gumbel on the *Today Show,* and had become convinced that NBC News would allow only one top black male anchor at the network.[14]

"We had this team, and we decided we would just be patient and watch the ratings books," explained Oprea.[15] Indeed, the ratings went up, although there were miscues. One involved anchorman Ben Frazier, one of the most intriguing "coulda-beens" in the history of Detroit television. He briefly coanchored Channel 4's 6:00 and 11:00 p.m. newscasts in 1980–81 with Mort Crim. Ratings were up. Frazier seemed to have it all: he had a self-assured style and a perfect broadcast voice. But then, as he told *Detroit Free Press* reporter Ellen Creager, he made some "pretty bad choices."[16] Acting on the advice of his agent, Frazier called in sick during the fall of 1981. The station thought—probably accurately—that Frazier was angling for a pay raise before his contract was up, and dismissed him. A controversy ensued; picketers at WDIV-TV insisted that Frazier's dismissal was a "racially motivated demotion and unconscionable treatment." Wrote *Detroit News* television writer Ben Brown: "It [the brouhaha] is not about people being dumped on. It's not about racism. It's not even about television. The issue is money. Frazier wants more of it; Channel 4 doesn't want to pay it."[17]

Carmen Harlan, Frazier's replacement, was a graduate of Mumford High School and the University of Michigan, and also a perfect rejoinder for critics who had charged that WDIV-TV had no Detroit connection. She joined WDIV-TV in 1978 after working as a newsreader at WWWW-FM. Post-Newsweek officials singled her out as a prospective anchorwoman, grooming her for the chair next to Mort Crim. As the audience estimates given in table 36 show (see appendix), the ratings success was slow to come. But by 1986 the station had gone from third to first place. The story can be told in the Arbitron numbers.

The station strategy was to hire competent journalists and keep them there. The station faced the image problem of being "outsiders" squarely by simply keeping journalists in their seats until viewers realized that Post-Newsweek had a commitment to Detroit. WDIV-TV's success was WJBK-TV's failure.

While WDIV-TV managed to successfully change course, WJBK-TV was running into problems. ABC's stations had navigated the new world of "information and people, not mere news," as ABC's O'Leary had described post-1970s television journalism. While WWJ-TV immolated itself during the late 1960s and 1970s, WJBK-TV was shooting itself in the foot.

The roots of WJBK-TV's troubles can be traced from the early 1970s. Consultants from McHugh and Hoffman had warned WJBK-TV executives about problems in the market as early as 1973. That year McHugh and Hoffman told its client, "[F]or the first time since 1968, Channel 2 is *not* the favorite television station in Detroit." Channel 7's strategy had taken hold. "The Bonds-Kelly combination, abetted by Ackerman, have made this Detroit's favorite early evening news, especially among the 18–34 year olds, and among women," wrote McHugh and Hoffman researchers. "Personalities dominate this newscast, and because the personalities are so strong, its fans perceive the newscast to be the best in terms of coverage and clarity." Even more daunting for WJBK-TV, the researchers wrote, "This study shows a serious loss of position for WJBK-TV vis a vis WXYZ-TV, but in the opinion of McHugh and Hoffman, Inc. *prompt, decisive* action by the management of Channel 2 can slow the trend, and result in eventual recapture of market dominance. It is important to remember, however, that image changes are difficult to reverse, and *Channel 7 has started a new trend.*"[18]

The researchers had even more hard news for Channel 2. Channel 7's gains were across all class lines (see appendix, table 37). As the numbers illustrate, WXYZ-TV could boast double-digit gains in each of four classes, and leadership in two of the four. A 2 percent gain in the remaining two classes would have given WXYZ-TV a clean sweep. McHugh and Hoffman counseled that "*we must regain the young, working class viewers, who now comprise a major part of Channel 7's strength.*"[19]

The McHugh and Hoffman researchers were also picking up a major surge in Bill Bonds's popularity. Bonds had distinguished himself at WXYZ-TV with his coverage of the riot. He was moved in 1969 to KABC-TV, the ABC-owned television station in Los Angeles, a bigger television market with the potential for greater rewards for the company. Bonds replaced anchorman Baxter Ward, who abandoned news to run for the post of Los Angeles mayor.[20] Although Bonds's stint at KABC-TV could not be characterized as a failure, it could not be regarded as a success, either. KNXT-TV, the CBS-owned television station in Los Angeles, still dominated the local news hours by late 1969. KNXT-TV had introduced its "Big News" concept earlier in the decade, and enjoyed Big Success. At peak viewing time, KNXT-TV had an audience of 479,000, according to Arbitron. KNBC-TV, the NBC-owned station in Los Angeles, had an audience of 238,000. Arbitron estimated Bonds's audience at 202,000.[21] The move was fraught with frustration for Bonds. KABC-TV had roughly one-third the number of camera crews on the streets compared to KNXT-TV and KNBC-TV. "It's the toughest place I've ever worked in," he told a reporter in 1970.[22] The next year Bonds was gone. One account said Bonds "asked KABC for a leave of absence and subsequently terminated his contract by mutual agreement."[23] The Bonds move was a lose-lose for ABC in both Los Angeles and Detroit. WXYZ-TV suffered from the move, and KABC-TV did not improve its position. McHugh and Hoffman researchers characterized Bonds's move to Los Angeles as a major misstep for WXYZ-TV. "Channel 7 was working for its competition by allowing the departure of Bill Bonds who was the second-ranking newscaster in the market and had every indication of increased popularity," a consultant wrote in one report.[24]

But Bonds returned, and caught on—in a big way. McHugh and Hoffman's estimates of newscaster popularity in metro Detroit are given in table 38 (see appendix). The figures show clearly that Le Goff had not lost any of his luster, but that Bonds had caught fire. The reading on WWJ-TV's Dean Miller was inconclusive because of Miller's recent arrival.

Ironically, many of WXYZ-TV's on-air news personalities had once worked at WJBK-TV. The WJBK-TV alumni roster at WXYZ-TV included anchors Jac Le Goff and John Kelly, weathercasters Marilyn Turner and Jerry Hodak, and reporter/anchor Jack McCarthy. Phil Dick, a WJBK-TV market researcher, characterized the early 1970s-era raid: "WXYZ-TV had decided, 'if you can't beat them, eat them,' so they did. Jack McCarthy was the first one. They found out how easy it was to do it so they decided to go after John Kelly. They just bought them off, piece-by-piece, diluting the product to a point where they didn't have to worry about it."[25]

Weathercaster Jerry Hodak was the first frontline player to leave WJBK-TV for WXYZ-TV. Kelly was the second, although the move had little to do with journalism and everything to do with Kelly's personal life. By 1972 Kelly felt that he "knew one thing—I had to get out! I don't know where or to what. I just couldn't stay and do what I had been doing. It was just too much. I was burned out."[26] Kelly hired Detroit attorney Henry Baskin to represent him in negotiations. Baskin was accustomed to high-stakes dealings in the show business world, representing such diverse talents as singer Marvin Gaye and the Temptations singing group. "When John Kelly wanted to leave Channel 2 and do something when his contract expired, Jerry [Hodak] told him to call me," remembered Baskin. An early feeler from Baskin on Kelly's behalf was rebuffed by WXYZ-TV's general manager, Donald F. Keck. Baskin went over his head and made a pitch to Richard O'Leary, president of ABC's owned-and-operated station division. Leary responded by offering Kelly $70,000 a year—more than double Kelly's $30,000 annual salary at WJBK-TV. "The idea was to destroy the [New York] Yankees [baseball team] by taking away their players—and incidentally gain some market share by putting them over at [Channel] 7," said Baskin.

It was a plan engineered out of New York. It was a plan developed and conceived to get the players off their [WJBK-TV's] team and send [them] off to different parts [of the country—or Channel 7. . . . Channel 2 didn't know what was happening. Channel 2 was backing and filling. . . . They [Storer] were making money, but they weren't willing to share it. ABC could spend double—and would spend double—to capture the market. . . . They realized they couldn't stop Channel 2 unless you took those people out of there. . . . This was not a random plan.[27]

After hiring anchorman John Kelly and weathercaster Marilyn Turner from WJBK-TV and picking up Al Ackerman from WWJ-TV, the station hired a Chicago advertising agency to design a campaign promoting the new employees. The Chicago advertising man who created the campaign, Joe Sedelmaier, built a career dreaming up zany television ads. (He later created the Wendy's "Where's the Beef?" promotion.) He had been hired by ABC executives to design a marketing campaign to sell the station's new news team. Sedelmaier employed the same madcap techniques that he later used to sell hamburgers. In WXYZ-TV spots, Sedelmaier featured two shady-looking characters "getting" whom the station wanted. The characters spirited Bill Bonds away from a movie theater; the same two characters hauled Marilyn Turner away in a telephone booth as she chatted with a friend, grabbed Ackerman as he covered a boxing match, and spirited Kelly out of an elevator. Promotion was not unusual in Detroit television news. Advertising in the past, however, was usually limited to simple messages in *TV Guide* or the television section of a newspaper. The WXYZ-TV campaign marked the first all-out effort in Detroit to pitch a journalistic product as entertainment. Sedelmaier's ads were seen on television, in newspapers, magazines, and on the sides of buses. Neither WJBK-TV nor WWJ-TV had tried that kind of promotion. Once again, it was the sizzle, not the steak, that was being sold.

The last to leave was Le Goff, who was hired by WXYZ-TV in mid-1974. Le Goff's new contract at WXYZ-TV paid $100,000 a year for ten years.[28]

McHugh and Hoffman researchers warned WJBK-TV the next year that the mass defection was a major problem for the station and would cost dearly. "The departure of Le Goff and Kelly from Channel 2 and their current pairing on Channel 7 seems to have made Channel 2 most vulnerable to viewer attitudes. *At present, Channel 2 ranks a distant second and Channel 4 in third position of preference,*" wrote researcher Philip L. McHugh. And there were other problems. McHugh wrote that Le Goff had "remerged as the dean of Detroit newscasters. . . . In part, he merits the position because of his long-standing service to the community, and the 'rocky up-and-down' road he has traveled moving from one to another of the channels, yet remaining in a high position as favorite newscaster." McHugh described viewer perceptions of Le Goff as "controlled, sophisticated and authoritative."[29]

McHugh described the key to the success of the Le Goff and Kelly team: "Their obvious skill, enthusiasm and enjoyment make the news a kind of showcase rather than a routine obligation or duty. This especially appeals to those who are not deeply news-oriented and to young viewers who identify with their vigor."[30]

McHugh's warning proved to be prescient. Table 39 presents data on WJBK-TV's news viewership from the mid- to late 1970s (see appendix). As can be seen, the station saw a drop-off of 41 percent at 6:00 p.m. between 1976 and 1979, and a 31 percent decrease between 1978 and 1979, the first year of Post-Newsweek's stewardship at WDIV-TV. Ratings were more than a beauty contest, since the numbers translated directly into dollars. As researcher Josef Steven Olsavsky was told while studying the Detroit television news market during the early 1980s, one rating point at 11:00 p.m. was worth $1 million.[31] Specifically, WXYZ-TV charged $1,000 for a thirty-second spot on its late afternoon/early evening newscast and $2,400 for a spot on its late newscast. At the same time, WDIV-TV charged $700 for a spot on its early news and $1,750 at 11:00 p.m. WJBK-TV charged $450 for thirty seconds during its early news, 45 percent of WXYZ-TV's take during the same time period. At 11:00 p.m., WJBK-TV charged $1,800 for a spot, two-thirds of WXYZ-TV's take.

The shift was viewed with some alarm by WJBK-TV's newsroom personnel. Reporter Murray Feldman, who joined the station in December 1976, recalls receiving a telephone call from one of his new supervisors, who proudly told Feldman: "Congratulations, you're coming to work at the station that's number one on every newscast we do—7 a.m., noon, 6 p.m. and 11 p.m." "We started to slip," Feldman says.

> We took it for granted that we were number one, and that was the way it would be. But it wasn't. And after we started to slip, we were told by management not to worry about it, because even if you're number two

you can still make more money than the number one station because they're spending a lot more money on marketing, whatever you want to break that into—maybe talent, maybe advertising, whatever. . . . What we didn't realize at the time: when you're number two, you're real close to number three. And it's hard to get back from number three. And that's what happened.[32]

Unfortunately for WJBK-TV, Channel 4 was about to come out of its slump. "Channel 4 could not get a live remote out of downtown Detroit," remembers Feldman. "They couldn't do it."[33] But WWJ-TV was about to get a new owner and new call letters—WDIV-TV—and after years of shuffling anchors and internal difficulties was about to turn itself around. Its new news team would catch on—after some painful experimentation.

With the numbers sagging, Storer Broadcasting brought Bill Flynn, who had been had been the company's "Mr. Fixit," to Detroit during the spring of 1982. Flynn had worked for Storer Broadcasting in Boston during the 1970s. He fixed the anemic ratings after grabbing broadcast rights to Boston Bruins hockey games—which shot through the roof as the team became a Stanley Cup contender during the late 1960s and early 1970s. (The team won a Stanley Cup championship in 1972 and played in the Stanley Cup finals at the end of the 1973–74 season.) Flynn later snared the television rights to Boston Red Sox baseball games by walking into negotiations with a $1 million check.[34] The negotiating ploy paid off when Boston won an American League pennant in 1975. Flynn managed a turnaround at Storer's Cleveland station. The company thought Flynn could work similar TV magic in Detroit, too. But Flynn's methods made him one of the most infamous TV station executives in Detroit.

Among the first to feel the heat from Flynn was anchorman Joe Glover, who joined the station in 1974. Although thoroughly professional, competent, and smooth, he never quite basked in the celebrity glow that surrounded contemporaries Bill Bonds and Mort Crim. Glover did the news and was proud of that. "I really thought that I at least tried not to cave in to the tendency of television news to lean towards show biz. I tried to be a journalist rather than a television personality," he said. "I always kind of resisted that. I always thought the story was more important. Maybe I was wrong. Maybe that's just the way television was going and they needed somebody to go out and get in fistfights."[35]

Glover grew up in Washington, DC, and in New England during World War II. He learned the craft of television in Seoul, Korea, where he broadcast news for the U.S. troops who remained after the end of the Korean War. Glover's early broadcast career is testimony to the gypsy life of a news broadcaster—Miami, Miami Beach, Jacksonville, West Palm Beach, New York City, New Orleans, San Francisco, and Sacramento.

WJBK-TV was in even deeper trouble with viewers by the late 1970s. A McHugh and Hoffman study of the Detroit television market in 1979 showed the weakness. "WXYZ-TV is the most popular station in Detroit—with a more than two-to-one margin of preference over WJBK-TV, the second favorite station," wrote researcher Peter S. Hoffman. "It should not be ignored, however, that fully one-third [of] the audience does not have a favorite station."[36] Still, the numbers were dismal for WJBK-TV (see appendix, table 40).

WXYZ-TV's news image was unassailable. Hoffman's researchers measured each station's news image in a dozen dimensions, including strength of the station's weather team and which station was considered "most reliable." Hoffman found that, for WXYZ-TV, "no area represents any significant weakness." While some viewers might criticize individual members of the WXYZ-TV news team, the station—planned or not—had found a way to mute that criticism. Wrote Hoffman: "While the fans of WXYZ-TV are highly enthusiastic about the newscasts and news personalities, there are openly expressed criticisms directed toward specific individuals (either Bonds, Kelly, Le Goff or Ackerman). However, because of the different combinations of news teams used, viewers can avoid the personality they particularly dislike, yet still enjoy all the aspects of the newscasts they like."[37]

Hoffman's research indicated that "there is no indication yet that he [Glover] is capable of challenging the market's leader, Bill Bonds." Worse yet, Hoffman wrote that viewers felt WJBK-TV's newscast lacked "pep and vitality," and that weathercaster Barry ZeVan and anchor Beverly Payne "annoy these viewers."[38]

Glover is candid about his weakness in the modern world of television. He admits he never put on much of a show for viewers. But he was fired by Flynn not because of any journalistic failings, but for an ancillary reason. "He had been here for some time when the station was on a downhill slide and he was part of the losers—not the man himself—but the loser image that comes with it," Flynn explained to researcher Olsavsky.[39]

Flynn also fired weathercaster Sonny Eliot, who had been on air for a part of each decade for the last five decades. Flynn had hired an outside research firm, Selection Research Institute, to divine Detroit viewer attitudes. When Flynn interpreted the numbers as negative, Eliot was called into Flynn's office immediately prior to a newscast and fired. The station was overwhelmed with nasty telephone calls, especially from viewers who were offended by the way Eliot was dismissed. Wrote *Detroit News* columnist Pete Waldmeir: "I'll wager that a lot of folks will long remember the cold unfeeling way Flynn gave Sonny the hook."[40]

In the end Flynn's mass firing did not work. Most insiders thought that Flynn misjudged viewer comfort levels. According to former anchorman Joe Glover:

[Channel] 7 was willing to spend tons of money. . . . They were an [ABC] o-and-o [owned-and-operated station], so they just had an unlimited budget. . . . Not only did they have all the familiar faces in town, they had all the money to promote them. . . . At the same time, [Channel] 2 was just shuffling around. The man I replaced was there less than a year. . . . You've got faces changing and unfamiliar faces on the air at Channel 2 and then, as this is all happening, Channel 4 is putting people in place and leaving them there. . . . 2 continued to change faces. . . . What stations do frequently, and as I remember this is kind of what happened at 2, they see what somebody else is doing, that's working well, they think, "Well, we should do that." But they forget that the people that are watching them are watching because they like what they're seeing. So they abandon those people, and at that same time they don't have the new people because the other place or places have them. If you do schlock news well, you do well in the numbers. If you do good, solid news well, you do well in the numbers. It's what you're putting into your product that serves you well. If you try to scrimp and save and just do it on a shoestring, no matter what you do—if you do quality news or schlock news—you won't do well in the numbers.[41]

What Glover seemed to be saying was that journalism was becoming less relevant in television news. Viewers wanted entertainment and thrills.

Perhaps nothing shows the nature of television news by the 1980s better than an examination of the career of Lee Thornton. She was educated, with an MA from Michigan State University and a PhD from Northwestern University. Her eight years at CBS News gave her excellent journalistic credentials. Despite the résumé, she came to grief in the world of local television news. Thornton lasted six months at WJBK-TV in 1982, a victim of the show business element of the industry.

After eight years as a CBS News correspondent, Thornton decided she had gone as far as she could at the network. She asked her agent to send out feelers to a few CBS affiliates. WJBK-TV's officials made an offer. An assistant news director took Thornton on a tour of the city. Thornton felt she might have a place in Detroit. She joined WJBK-TV in February 1982 as anchor of its 6:00 and 11:00 p.m. newscasts. Thornton recalled later that her intentions were simple: "I wanted to do well at work that I enjoyed, build a career and a life. Just about what anybody wants whatever they do! I did not come there knowing as much as perhaps I ought to have known about that city—but I'm a pretty quick study and I thought, with time, I would find my way journalistically, turn up good stories and grow into things, grow into the station 'family' and grow into the city."[42]

Within a month the two men who had hired her had been fired. But what ended her Detroit television career was an overly ambitious on-air promotion campaign enumerating her impressive résumé and stressing her work at CBS News and her education. Instead of appearing as a well-credentialed journalist ready to do a job, she came off as a snooty outsider, the "pro from Dover," who was going to show Detroit how it was done. Thornton recalls how the spot came about:

> I was taken to a soundstage and asked to read some copy into the camera. Okay. I can do that. I never saw the spot before it went on air and there was this voice as if from on high screaming my name and credentials— and there I was prattling about myself into the camera. Oh, good Lord. It was awful. And it aired in high saturation during the Super Bowl local access that year. I knew instantly that it was a disaster. I had friends, the wife worked at city hall, she called me and said people were calling city hall saying, essentially, "Who does this b—— think she is?" I had no idea I was coming to a place as xenophobic as all of that. It was pretty brutal.[43]

The appearance had nothing to do with the reality of Thornton's attitudes. That did not matter. As *Detroit News* television critic Ben Brown described the promotion, "There she was in down-to-business furrowed brow, striding into a studio foreground." Brown continued: "The arrogance would have been hard to swallow anywhere, but in xenophobic Detroit, where outsiders have to pay heavy dues before they get bragging rights, the promo was unpardonable."[44]

Thornton felt that she was living in a "zoo." She asked to be let out of her contract. "I knew a short time into this experience that whatever I'd thought I would accomplish there would not be possible," she later wrote. Thornton negotiated a small payout—enough to move her belongings back to Washington, DC, and a few months of salary. She later remembered it as "surely the longest five months of my life."[45]

In the end, her journalistic credentials meant nothing. What mattered was the promotion behind her appearance. She failed because of a sloppy, ill-conceived promotional campaign. Although McHugh and Hoffman were no longer working for WJBK-TV, it is clear where the flaw in the station's promotional campaign lay: McHugh and Hoffman had preached tailoring newscasts to Joe Six-Pack. WJBK-TV's campaign centered on Thornton's elite credentials. The 28 percent of adults over the age of twenty-five who had a college education might appreciate Thornton's résumé. But the other 72 percent might just resent it.

The changes that hit WDIV-TV were only the beginning of ownership change in Detroit television. Both WJBK-TV and WXYZ-TV were sold during the same week. In each case, the ownership changes were a result of bigger shifts in the national television world.

WXYZ-TV went on the auction block after Capital Cities Communications, Inc. bought the American Broadcasting Companies for $3.4 billion.[1] The announcement was made in March 1985. As part of the acquisition, the newly formed company sold properties to comply with Federal Communications Commission regulations. The Scripps Howard Broadcasting Company bought WXYZ-TV and WFTS-TV in Tampa for $246 million. Former ABC and Capital Cities radio and television stations, along with the firm's cable systems, were peddled for a total of $650 million.[2]

That's where the ownership turmoil stopped for WXYZ-TV. But WJBK-TV went through much, much more—a victim of the shifting vicissitudes of various entrepreneurs. Storer Communications was sold to Kohlberg, Kravis, Roberts, & Company (KKR) in July 1985 for $2.51 billion.[3] Within two years KKR sold a 51 percent interest in the Storer Group to Denver businessman George Gillett Jr. Gillett had had a diverse career before getting into the television business.[4] He had managed the Miami Dolphins and Harlem Globetrotters, and also owned a Nashville meatpacking plant. By the mid-1980s his intention was to build a television chain by boosting local news ratings and controlling costs.[5] Gillett got control of the Storer stations for $1.3 billion. At one point Congressman Edward Markey expressed concern that Gillett was trying to dodge FCC regulations capping the number of television stations a broadcaster could own.

However, Gillett built his empire on debt—which put the company in play and eventually sank it altogether. At one juncture Gillett and KKR had an agreement to sell the company to Lorimar-Telepictures Corporation, which produced high-profile network television shows such as *Dallas*. Lorimar announced it would buy the Storer Stations for $1.85 billion in May 1986, but backed out of the deal six months later.[6] By 1993

Gillett's SCI Television Inc. was $1.3 billion in the red. Investor Ronald O. Perelman, whose business interests ranged from Revlon makeup products to Marvel Comics, bought a 51 percent stake in Gillett's company for a mere $100 million.

Perelman engineered what is arguably the biggest change in the history of Detroit television. WJBK-TV had been the city's only CBS affiliate since the beginning of television. Fox network owner Rupert Murdoch was eager to obtain better dial positions for his new fledgling television network. He talked Perelman into a deal: switch the affiliation of the New World stations to Fox in exchange for a $500 million Fox investment in New World. WJBK-TV made the change from CBS to Fox in 1994. It was part of a major repositioning that involved stations in Dallas, Atlanta, Cleveland, Phoenix, and elsewhere moving to television's newest network.[7] The other shoe dropped two years later. Perelman and media magnate Rupert Murdoch had talked about Fox buying New World outright. Perelman held firm until Fox agreed to buy New World Communications for $3.4 billion, making WJBK-TV a Fox owned-and-operated station.[8] There is no record of Perelman ever having visited WJBK-TV.

That left CBS, Inc. in search of a local Detroit outlet, so the company bought WGPR-TV in 1995 for $22 million.[9] The sale had national implications. WGPR-TV was the first African American–owned television station in the country. The president of the CBS-owned station group told inquiring reporters that the station would build a news department, and would either build a new headquarters or make a major real estate investment in the city of Detroit.[10] The company reneged on both promises. CBS was to undergo its own ownership changes. When the company took control of Detroit's WKBD-TV, the company pulled the plug on that station's newscast.

WDIV-TV settled into a successful routine, and reaped rewards for its consistency. Crim stayed at the anchor desk with Carmen Harlan, sportscaster Bernie Smilovitz, and weathercaster Chuck Gaidica.

It is here that Daniel J. Boorstin's analysis is depressingly correct. "We need not be theologians to see that we have shifted responsibility for making the world interesting from God to the newspaperman," Boorstin wrote in his groundbreaking book, *The Image: A Guide to Pseudo-Events in America.*[11] He referred to newspapers, but his admonition could easily be applied to what happened to Detroit television in the 1980s and 1990s.

If Detroit television viewers wanted entertainment, they got it. The life of anchorman Bill Bonds turned into a soap opera, with Detroit's two major newspapers chronicling his escapades, both on air and off air, and sometimes covering local television the way the *National Enquirer* covers Hollywood. (The author, a television writer at the *Detroit News* between 1990 and 2002, was among the gossipmongering scribes.)

An inconsequential brawl in a Southfield saloon in 1988 landed Bill Bonds back on the front page of the *Detroit News*.[12] An arrest for driving with a suspended license the previous year also received publicity.[13] Bonds, apparently under the influence of alcohol while anchoring on a July 14, 1989, newscast, challenged Detroit mayor Coleman Young to a fistfight.[14] The challenge, of course, was played on the front page of the *Detroit News*. Bonds appeared often on the front page of the newspaper during the next six weeks. His entry into a Los Angeles substance abuse program made the front page of the paper, as did his return to the airwaves in late August.[15] Columnists Pete Waldmeir, Chuck Moss, and Laura Berman all opined on the topic. In total, Bonds received eighteen mentions in the pages of the *News* that year and twenty-two in the *Detroit Free Press*.[16]

A subsequent drunk-driving arrest in 1994 kept him on the front page for three days running: his arrest made the front page on August 8, an announcement that he would take a leave of absence appeared there on August 9, and his entry to a substance abuse clinic again made the front page on August 10.[17] The results of his blood alcohol test, in which he weighed in with a .21 blood alcohol level, received prominent display on the front of the newspaper's local section on August 18. He was again on the front page on December 2, when he pleaded guilty to a drunk-driving charge.

Bonds was not the only one to suffer disgrace. WJBK-TV officials pulled morning anchorman Warren Pierce off the air during fall 1995 for violation of the station's ethics policies.[18] That story, as well as subsequent ones giving details of the violation and his dismissal, hit the front page.[19]

Bonds took his "Brawling Billy" persona to an extreme. On October 16, 1991, he engaged in a verbal mud-wrestling match with Senator Orrin Hatch (R-UT). A transcript of the interview shows an out-of-control anchorman who seemed to be more interested in heat than light.

> Bonds: I have to say to you, sir, just as an American from the Midwest, that frankly, you and your colleagues on the Senate Judiciary Committee—

with some of your cheap shots at one another—that was kind of an embarrassing spectacle. Do you regret that that went on?

Hatch: Well, I didn't see any real cheap shots. You know it was a tense, difficult process, as it should be. And it was made even worse because of one dishonest senator who leaked raw FBI data that then became public.

Bonds: Senator, you guys leak all the time.

Hatch: No, that's not true.

Bonds: Who are you trying to kid? You guys leak stuff all the time.

Hatch: Let me just say something, that's not true.

Bonds: Yes it is.

Hatch: No, not FBI reports from the Judiciary Committee. Look, I've been there fifteen years. I know what's going on.

Bonds: There are guys who say you've been there too long.

Hatch: That could be. In fifteen years, I have not seen leaks of FBI reports because they contain raw data. They contain raw information of people who are crazy, people who hate each other, people who have axes to grind, and that's why they don't do that, and we've always honored that. This time they did not. And the bad thing was that everybody knew about this report before the vote. Senator Biden had explained it to every Democrat. Everybody on the committee, each person could have put it over for a week.

Bonds: OK, your conduct was great. You guys all look terrific. Two hundred fifty million Americans are really proud of Senator Orrin Hatch and all the rest of you guys.

Hatch: I'm not, I'm not . . .

Bonds: You did a marvelous job, we're all proud of you. You never made the country look better. Let me ask you something: What are you going to do if you find out six months from now that Clarence Thomas, who you've just about made into a saint, is a porno freak?

Hatch: Don't worry, we won't. But I'll tell you: If you're going to interview us in the future, you ought to be at least courteous. I think you're about as discourteous a person as I've ever, ever interviewed with. I don't like you, and I don't like what you are doing. If you don't like what we're saying, if you don't like what we're doing, then say so. But don't act that way with me.

Bonds: Well, I didn't vote for you, Senator.

Hatch: Well, I appreciate that. But don't act like that with me. Look, I go through enough crap back here, I don't have to go through it with you. Let me tell you something.

Bonds: No, let me tell you something . . .

Hatch: No, you tell yourself something. I'm tired of talking to you.

Bonds: OK, fine. I'm tired of talking to you. See you later.[20]

The new content during this period consisted of one car crash after another. The author conducted a content analysis of two weeks of Detroit television news in late 1996 and early 1997. The late newscasts of WJBK-TV, WDIV-TV, WXYZ-TV, and WKBD-TV were analyzed (see appendix, table 41). As the table illustrates, Detroit television news by 1997 was heavy with crime and disaster. "Every night, people are getting the same kind of terrifying, titillating, sensationalism. They are manipulating us. Hyping it, overblowing it—all in the pursuit of ratings," said Paul Klite, executive director of Rocky Mountain Media Watch, a Denver-based independent news consumer group. "And you wonder why people are becoming cynical."[21]

● ● ●

What started out as a publicity ploy (as author Sally Bedell Smith so aptly put it) had developed into something quite grand—and lucrative.[22] Television and radio news both showed flashes of brilliance as the media developed. But as money became important, journalism became less so. Former CBS News president Bill Leonard wrote about the choice of CBS News anchorman Dan Rather as anchorman of the *CBS Evening News* in 1980. Leonard had agreed to a contract with Rather, but had to get agreement from the company's most senior officials. CBS, Inc. president John Backe balked at Rather's price tag, which was $22 million over a ten-year period. There was no discussion whatsoever about Rather's qualifications for the job or his journalistic abilities, as there had been when Walter Cronkite had gotten the job twenty years earlier.[23]

After some debate, CBS chairman William S. Paley wrote the following phrase on a memo pad: "1 point = $5 million."[24] That, it would seem, is what journalism has come to, both on the network level and on the local level. The money has become so overwhelmingly important to television news officials that show business triumphs over traditional journalistic values.

Edward R. Murrow saw the problem clearly: "I am frightened by the imbalance, the constant striving to reach the largest possible audience for everything; by the absence of a sustained study of the state of the nation. Heywood Broun once said, 'No body politic is healthy until it begins to itch.' I would like television to produce some itching pills, rather than this endless outpouring of tranquilizers. It can be done."[25]

Murrow had it partly wrong. Local television news is less an "outpouring of tranquilizers" than an outpouring of thrills. It is not hard to see how that happened. Network television and syndicated programming began gobbling up more and more local television time. By 1962 the networks had taken up two-thirds of the broadcast day on a typical station. During the late 1980s and 1990s, syndicated television program such as *Oprah Winfrey* and *Judge Judy* gobbled up much of the rest. That left television stations with local news as the main revenue stream.

Local television news has painted itself into a corner. At a time when it took up an hour of a television station's schedule, it may have been easier to live with mediocre ratings. But this is no longer the case. In order to maintain healthy profit margins, the stations have to reach the largest possible audience. With cable television and the Internet now competing for the attention of a viewer with an appetite for news, the pressure on local television news to produce ratings has become even more intense.

The McHugh and Hoffman firm hit on something: produce a newscast for the masses. But nobody raised the question: What if what audiences want is a circus? What if they want entertainment-based news?

It is appropriate to raise a philosophical question here. Should journalism put itself in a popularity contest, as it has so clearly done? As this book shows, local television began applying show business techniques to news in the late 1960s. Although entertainment values were present in radio news from the beginning, entertainment was not the primary motive of radio. Nor was entertainment the primary motive in either local or network news. That happened only later, when station managers began to look at news as a source of revenue.

The two motives are at odds with each other. As Murrow pointed out, journalists are not in the business of being popular. They are, or should be, in the business of being annoying. Some can do both. Joseph Pulitzer, for instance, had a talent for selling newspapers while also providing valuable public service with his investigations. What local television news has provided, for the most part, is an eye-popping television program.

Ultimately, the viewers make the choice. The reason broadcasters air the kind of news they do is because people watch. Nielsen Media Research provides ratings each morning for the Detroit market, breaking down audience viewing patterns in fifteen-minute increments. McHugh and Hoffman did its job well, giving WJBK-TV a road map to the desires of Detroit viewers, and WXYZ-TV figured out a way to extend the franchise further out. Ultimately, the stations may be providing the viewers with exactly what they want.

Table 1. Percentage of people who regularly watch various news media, 1993–2006

General categories	1993	1996	2000	2002	2004	2006
Local TV news	77	65	56	57	59	54
Cable TV news				33	38	34
Nightly network news	60	42	30	32	34	28
Network morning shows			20	22	22	23

Source: "Online Papers Modestly Boost Newspaper Readership," survey of 3,204 adults from April 27 to May 22, 2006, for the Pew Research Center for the People and the Press, July 30, 2006, http://www.people-press.org.

Table 2. Percentage of TV station revenue produced by news, 2006

Market rank	Average	Median	Minimum	Maximum	Not sure
All TV news	44.9	45.0	0	85.0	75.0
Market ranks 1–25	36.2	40.0	10.0	60.0	75.8
Market ranks 26–50	41.7	40.0	0	85.0	74.5
Market ranks 51–100	48.7	50.0	30.0	70.0	73.8
Market ranks 101–50	48.3	42.0	25.0	70.0	74.0
Market ranks 151+	43.3	50.0	10.0	60.0	78.6

Source: Radio-Television News Directors Association, Communicator, October 2006, 30, http://www.rtnda/.org/research.

Table 3. Newspaper companies involved in early television broadcasting, 1946

Company	TV station	Newspaper
A. S. Abell Co.	WMAR	Baltimore Sun
Carter Publications, Inc.	KCPN	Fort Worth Star-Telegram
Chronicle Publishing Co.	KCPR	San Francisco Chronicle
Courier-Journal & Louisville Times Co.	WHAS	Louisville Courier-Journal
Evening News Association	WWJ	Detroit News
Evening Star Broadcasting Co.	WTVW	Evening Star (Washington, DC)
Hearst Radio, Inc.	WWBT	Baltimore News-American
Oregonian Publishing Co.	WGWG	Oregonian
Philadelphia Inquirer	WFIL	Philadelphia Inquirer
Pulitzer Publishing Co.	KSD	St. Louis Post-Dispatch
WBEN, Inc.	WBEN	Buffalo Evening News

Source: "Licensees and CP's as of October 1, 1946," *Broadcasting & Telecasting*, October 7, 1946, 39.

Table 4. ABC revenue and income, networks and owned stations, 1953–55

Year	1953	1954	1955
Network revenue	$12,399,727	$24,750,893	$33,234,630
Network expenses	$16,783,526	$31,573,978	$32,753,492
Network earnings	($4,383,799)	($6,823,085)	$481,138
Owned station revenue	$17,853,653	$19,768,165	$20,671,850
Owned station expenses	$15,375,575	$15,449,342	$15,563,536
Owned station earnings	$2,478,078	$4,318,823	$5,108,314
Broadcast earnings	($1,905,721)	($2,504,862)	$5,589,452

Source: *Television Factbook, Spring–Summer 1957* (Washington, DC: Television Digest, 1957), 45.

Table 5. CBS revenue and income, networks and owned stations, 1953–55

Year	1953	1954	1955
Network revenue	$68,067,235	$97,394,599	$121,953,917
Network expenses	$63,190,112	$84,293,430	$101,588,539
Network earnings	$4,877,123	$13,101,169	$20,365,378
Owned station revenue	$19,089,071	$25,809,248	$31,660,400
Owned station expenses	$12,081,041	$13,532,805	$17,154,941
Owned station earnings	$7,008,030	$12,276,443	$14,505,459
Broadcast earnings	$11,885,153	$25,377,612	$34,870,837

Source: *Television Factbook, Spring–Summer 1957* (Washington, DC: Television Digest, 1957), 45.

Table 6. NBC revenue and income, networks and owned stations, 1953–55

Year	1953	1954	1955
Network revenue	$73,764,819	$90,671,284	$124,353,526
Network expenses	$73,382,508	$86,653,388	$109,750,710
Network earnings	$382,111	$4,017,898	$14,602,816
Owned station revenue	$24,403,611	$29,713,971	$34,690,627
Owned station expenses	$15,939,389	$17,695,577	$19,114,094
Owned station earnings	$8,464,222	$12,018,394	$15,576,533
Broadcast earnings	$8,846,333	$16,086,290	$30,179,349

Source: *Television Factbook, Spring–Summer 1957* (Washington, DC: Television Digest, 1957), 45.

Table 7. DuMont revenue and income, networks and owned stations, 1953–55

Year	1953	1954	1955
Network revenue	$7,070,868	$8,300,941	$2,862,867
Network expenses	$10,878,230	$13,441,002	$4,384,722
Network earnings	($3,807,362)	($5,140,061)	($1,521,863)
Owned station revenue	$9,019,562	$10,267,552	$4,612,955
Owned station expenses	$6,030,622	$7,414,757	$5,661,708
Owned station earnings	$2,988,940	$2,852,795	($1,048,753)
Broadcast earnings	($818,422)	($2,287,266)	($2,570,618)

Source: *Television Factbook, Spring–Summer 1957* (Washington, DC: Television Digest, 1957), 45.

Table 8. Income and investment, ABC stations, 1955

Station	Broadcast income	New investment in tangible property	Ratio of income to investment
WXYZ-TV, Detroit	$1,540,074	$330,479	4.66
WBKB-TV, Chicago	$1,668,516	$919,568	1.81
WABC-TV, New York	$740,590	$2,793,990	.27
KGO-TV, San Francisco	$624,368	$1,366,583	.46
KABC-TV, Los Angeles	$534,766	$1,161,007	.46

Source: U.S. Congress, House Committee on the Judiciary, Antitrust Subcommittee, *The Television Broadcasting Industry*, 85th Cong., 1st sess., 1957, 31–32.

Table 9. Income and investment, ABC stations, 1954

Station	Broadcast income	New investment in tangible property	Ratio of income to investment
WXYZ-TV, Detroit	$1,243,586	$239,000	5.20
WBKB-TV, Chicago	$1,849,441	$341,722	5.41
WABC-TV, New York	$642,379	$3,437,876	.10
KGO-TV, San Francisco	$474,044	$442,038	1.07
KABC-TV, Los Angeles	$109,373	$1,320,646	.08

Source: U.S. Congress, House Committee on the Judiciary, Antitrust Subcommittee, *The Television Broadcasting Industry*, 85th Cong., 1st sess., 1957, 31–32.

Table 10. Income and investment, ABC stations, 1953

Station	Broadcast income	New investment in tangible property	Ratio of income to investment
WXYZ-TV, Detroit	$1,445,331	$357,899	4.04
WBKB-TV, Chicago	$1,636,439	$386,143	4.24
WABC-TV, New York	($478,478)	$3,443,624	
KGO-TV, San Francisco	$490,137	$468,221	1.05
KABC-TV, Los Angeles	($615,571)	$1,431,942	

Source: U.S. Congress, House Committee on the Judiciary, Antitrust Subcommittee, *The Television Broadcasting Industry*, 85th Cong., 1st sess., 1957, 31–32.

Table 11. WJBK-TV local newscasts, 1950–59

Date	Time slot	Minutes	Total
July 6, 1950[a]	5 p.m.	:15	
	6 p.m.	:10	
	10 p.m.	:15	40 minutes
December 20, 1951[b]	10 a.m.	:15	
	11 a.m.	:15	
	6:30 p.m.	:15	
	11 p.m.	:10	55 minutes
March 20, 1952[c]	12:45 p.m.	:15	
	5:30 p.m.	:15	
	6:30 p.m.	:15	
	11 p.m.	:10	55 minutes
March 26, 1953[d]	6:30 p.m.	:15	
	11 p.m.	:15	30 minutes
June 17, 1954[e]	10 p.m.	:15	
	11 p.m.	:15	30 minutes
January 6, 1955[f]	8:25 a.m.	:05	
	6:30 p.m.	:15	
	11 p.m.	:15	35 minutes
November 21, 1956[g]	9:45 a.m.	:15	
	6 p.m.	:25	
	11 p.m.	:15	55 minutes
March 13, 1957[h]	9:45 a.m.	:10	
	1:55 p.m.	:05	
	6 p.m.	:15	
	11 p.m.	:15	45 minutes
February 27, 1958[i]	9:20 a.m.	:10	
	6:30 p.m.	:10	
	11 p.m.	:20	40 minutes
September 17, 1959[j]	6:30 p.m.	:15	
	11 p.m.	:10	25 minutes

Sources:
a. *TV Today*, July 1–7, 1950, 12–13.
b. *TV Today* December 15, 1951, 16.
c. *Detroit TV Weekly*, March 16, 1952, 22–23.
d. *TV Today*, March 21–27, 1953, 22, 24.
e. *TV Today*, June 11–17, 1954, 12, 20.
f. *TV Today*, December 31–January 6, 1955, 9, 20, 23.
g. *TV Guide*, November 17–23, 1956, A32–A34.
h. *Detroit News*, March 13, 1957, 60.
i. *TV Guide*, February 22–28, 1958, A48–A55.
j. *TV Guide*, September 12–18, 1959, A54–A58.

Table 12. WWJ-TV local newscasts, 1950–59

Date	Time slot	Minutes	Total
July 6, 1950[a]	11:30 p.m.		
December 20, 1951[b]	10:50 a.m.	:10	
	12:45 p.m.	:10	
	6:30 p.m.	:15	
	11 p.m.	:15	50 minutes
March 20, 1952[c]	6:50 a.m.	:10	
	9:45 a.m.	:10	
	6:30 p.m.	:15	
	11 p.m.	:15	50 minutes
March 26, 1953[d]	8:25 a.m.	:05	
	12 p.m.	:10	
	6:15 p.m.	:15	
	6:30 p.m.	:15	
	11 p.m.	:15	60 minutes
June 17, 1954[e]	11 p.m.	:15	15 minutes
January 6, 1955[f]	6:15 p.m.	:10	
	11 p.m.	:15	25 minutes
November 21, 1956[g]	6 p.m.	:15	
	11 p.m.	:15	30 minutes
March 13, 1957[h]	7:25 a.m.	:05	
	7:55 a.m.	:05	
	8:25 a.m.	:05	
	6:30 p.m.	:15	
	11 p.m.	:15	45 minutes
February 27, 1958[i]	6 p.m.	:15	
	6:20 p.m.	:10	
	11 p.m.	:20	45 minutes
September 17, 1959[j]	6 p.m.	:10	
	11:15 p.m.	:15	
	1 a.m.	:15	40 minutes

Sources:
a. *TV Today*, July 1–7, 1950, 12–13.
b. *TV Today*, December 15, 1951, 16.
c. *Detroit TV Weekly*, March 16, 1952, 22–23.
d. *TV Today*, March 21–27, 1953, 12, 22, 24.
e. *TV Today*, June 11–17, 1954, 12, 20.
f. *TV Today*, December 31–January 6, 1955, 9, 20, 23.
g. *TV Guide*, November 17–23, 1956, A32–A34.
h. *Detroit News*, March 13, 1957, 60.
i. *TV Guide*, February 22–28, 1958, A48–A55.
j. *TV Guide*, September 12–18, 1959, A52–A58.

Table 13. WXYZ-TV local newscasts, 1950–59

Date	Time slot	Minutes	Total
July 6, 1950[a]	None	:00	0 minutes
December 20, 1951[b]	11 p.m.	:10	10 minutes
March 20, 1952[c]	11 p.m.	:10	10 minutes
March 26, 1953[d]	8:55 a.m.	:05	
	12:55 p.m.	:05	
	2:55 p.m.	:05	
	4:55 p.m.	:05	
	5:55 p.m.	:05	
	6 p.m.	:30	55 minutes
June 10, 1954[e]	9 a.m.	:05	
	4:40 p.m.	:05	
	6 p.m.	:15	
	6:15 p.m.	:15	40 minutes
January 6, 1955[f]	8:55 a.m.	:05	
	11:55 a.m.	:05	
	3:55 p.m.	:05	15 minutes
November 21, 1956[g]	None	:00	0 minutes
March 13, 1957[h]	10:45 p.m.	:15	15 minutes
February 27, 1958[i]	11:25 a.m.	:05	5 minutes
September 17, 1959[j]	10:55 a.m.	:05	5 minutes

Sources:
a. *TV Today* July 1–7, 1950, 12–13.
b. *TV Today*, December 15, 1951, 16.
c. *Detroit TV Weekly*, March 16, 1952, 22–23.
d. *TV Today*, March 21–27, 1953, 12, 22, 24.
e. *TV Today*, June 4–11, 1954, 12, 20.
f. *TV Today*, December 31–January 6, 1955, 9, 20, 23.
g. *TV Guide*, November 17–23, 1956, A32–A34.
h. *Detroit News*, March 13, 1957, 60.
i. *TV Guide*, February 22–28, 1958, A48–A55.
j. *TV Guide*, September 12–18, 1959, A52–A58.

Table 14. Detroit radio revenue and income, 1948–58

Year	Number of stations	Revenue	% change	Expenses	% change	Net income	% change
1948	—	—	—	—	—	—	—
1949	8	$7,523,024	—	$5,288,843	—	$2,234,181	—
1950	—	—	—	—	—	—	—
1951	8	$7,485,039	—	$5,555,989	—	$1,929,050	—
1952	8	$7,161,437	-4.3	$5,431,404	-2.2	$1,730,033	-10.3
1953	8	$7,593,303	6.0	$5,668,009	4.4	$1,925,294	11.3
1954	—	—	—	—	—	—	—
1955	9	$6,363,947	—	$4,694,146	—	$1,669,801	—
1956	10	$9,125,271	43.4	$6,029,768	28.5	$3,095,503	85.4
1957	10	$10,186,376	11.6	$6,625,802	9.9	$3,560,574	15.0
1958	11	$9,418,810	-7.5	$6,912,207	4.3	$2,506,603	-29.6
1959	10	$10,294,887	9.3	$7,236,054	4.7	$3,058,833	22.0

Source: FCC, "Broadcast Revenues, Expenses and Income (Before Federal Income Tax) of the Radio Broadcast Service," available at the Library of American Broadcasting, University of Maryland, College Park.

Table 15. National radio revenue and income, all networks and stations, 1948–58

Year	Revenue (millions)	% change	Expenses (millions)	% change	Net income (millions)	% change
1948[a]	$408.1		$347.1		$61.0	
1949[b]	$415.2	1.7	$362.6	4.5	$52.6	-13.8
1950[c]	$444.5	7.1	$376.3	3.8	$68.2	29.7
1951[d]	$450.4	1.3	$392.9	4.4	$57.5	-15.7
1952[e]	$469.7	4.3	$409.6	4.3	$60.1	4.5
1953[f]	$475.3	1.2	$420.3	2.6	$55.0	-8.5
1954[g]	$449.5	-5.4	$407.7	-3.0	$41.8	-24.0
1955[h]	$453.4	0.9	$407.4	-0.1	$46.0	10.0
1956[i]	$480.6	6.0	$431.4	5.9	$49.2	7.0
1957[j]	$517.9	7.8	$463.3	7.4	$54.6	11.0
1958[k]	$523.1	1.0	$485.8	4.9	$37.3	-31.7

Sources:
a. FCC, *Fifteenth Report* (Washington, DC: GPO, 1950), 51, 52, 54.
b. FCC, *Sixteenth Report* (Washington, DC: GPO, 1951), 118.
c. FCC, *Seventeenth Report* (Washington, DC: GPO, 1952), 130.
d. FCC, *Eighteenth Report* (Washington, DC: GPO, 1953), 123.
e. FCC, *Nineteenth Report* (Washington, DC: GPO, 1954), 114.
f. FCC, *Twentieth Report* (Washington, DC: GPO, 1955), 110.
g. FCC, *Twenty First Report* (Washington, DC: GPO, 1956), 120.
h. FCC, *Twenty Second Report* (Washington, DC: GPO, 1957), 122.
i. FCC, *Twenty Third Report* (Washington, DC: GPO, 1958), 132.
j. FCC, *Twenty Fourth Report* (Washington, DC: GPO, 1959), 133. Later revised in FCC, *Twenty Fifth Report* (Washington, DC: GPO, 1960), 76.
k. FCC, *Twenty Fifth Report* (Washington, DC: GPO, 1960), 76.

Table 16. National television broadcast revenue and income, all networks and stations, 1948–58

Year	Revenue (millions)	% change	Expenses (millions)	% change	Net income (millions)	% change
1948[a]	$8.7		$23.6		-$14.9	
1949[b]	$34.3	294.3	$59.6	152.5	-$25.3	-70.0
1950[c]	$105.9	208.7	$115.1	93.1	-$9.2	63.6
1951[d]	$235.7	122.6	$194.1	68.6	$41.6	552.2
1952[e]	$324.2	37.5	$268.7	38.4	$55.5	33.4
1953[f]	$432.7	33.4	$364.7	35.7	$68.0	22.5
1954[g]	$593.0	37.0	$502.7	37.8	$90.3	32.8
1955[h]	$744.7	25.6	$594.5	18.3	$150.2	66.3
1956[i]	$896.9	20.4	$707.3	19.0	$189.6	26.2
1957[j]	$943.2	5.2	$783.2	10.7	$160.0	-15.6
1958[k]	$1,030.0	9.2	$858.1	9.6	$171.9	7.4

Sources:
a. FCC, *Fifteenth Report* (Washington, DC: GPO, 1950), 54.
b. FCC, *Sixteenth Report* (Washington, DC: GPO, 1951), 118.
c. FCC, *Seventeenth Report* (Washington, DC: GPO, 1952), 130.
d. FCC, *Eighteenth Report* (Washington, DC: GPO, 1953), 123.
e. FCC, *Nineteenth Report* (Washington, DC: GPO, 1954), 114.
f. FCC, *Twentieth Report* (Washington, DC: GPO, 1955), 110.
g. FCC, *Twenty First Report* (Washington, DC: GPO, 1956), 120.
h. FCC, *Twenty Second Report* (Washington, DC: GPO, 1957), 122.
i. FCC, *Twenty Third Report* (Washington, DC: GPO, 1958), 132.
j. FCC, *Twenty Fourth Report* (Washington, DC: GPO, 1959), 133.
k. FCC, *Twenty Fifth Report* (Washington, DC: GPO, 1960), 76.

Table 17. Detroit television broadcast revenue and income, 1950–59

Year	Revenue	% change	Expenses	% change	Net income	% change
1950	$3,059,000		—		—	
1951	$6,765,000	121.2	—	—	—	—
1952	$8,888,000	31.4	—	—	—	—
1953	$11,041,000	24.2	$6,215,000	—	$4,826,000	—
1954	$12,523,110	13.4	$6,812,250	9.6	$5,710,860	18.3
1955	—	—	—	—	—	—
1956	—	—	—	—	—	—
1957	$15,767,107	—	$8,266,803	—	$7,500,304	—
1958	$15,897,967	0.8	$8,673,495	4.9	$7,224,472	-3.7
1959	$17,448,502	9.8	$9,774,506	12.7	$7,673,996	6.2

Source: FCC, "Broadcast Revenues, Expenses and Income (Before Federal Income Tax) of the Radio Broadcast Service," available at the Library of American Broadcasting, University of Maryland, College Park.

Table 18. Network use of television time, 1953–62

Survey date	Average hours per week	% of total schedule
June 1953	48:11	51.6
December 1953	39:31	49.6
March 1955	47:45	50.7
October 1955	51:49	52.8
March 1956	57:23	55.8
October 1956	59:33	56.3
March 1957	60:44	57.4
October 1957	63:35	59.4
June 1958	59:02	52.5
June 1959	66:10	59.8
June 1960	68:07	63.1
June 1961	67:14	62.3
June 1962	69:57	62.7

Source: *Broadcasting Yearbook* (Washington, DC: Broadcasting, 1963), 19.

Table 19. Detroit Newspaper Circulation, 1949–59

Year	Detroit Free Press daily	% change	Detroit Free Press Sunday	% change	Detroit News daily	% change	Detroit News Sunday	% change	Detroit Times daily	% change	Detroit Times Sunday	% change
1949[a]	436,408		466,920		442,977		550,957		421,752		609,957	
1950[b]	449,449	3.0	473,004	1.3	452,760	2.2	560,158	1.7	440,317	4.4	604,779	-0.8
1951[c]	447,688	-0.4	471,502	-0.3	459,808	1.6	565,718	1.0	439,139	-0.3	600,567	-0.7
1952[d]	433,624	-3.1	455,132	-3.5	457,930	-0.4	559,134	-1.2	414,942	-5.5	563,957	-6.1
1953[e]	407,504	-6.0	435,738	-4.3	443,791	-3.1	544,622	-2.6	403,113	-2.9	535,720	-5.0
1954[f]	456,261	12.0	485,172	11.3	442,656	-0.3	549,629	0.9	411,611	2.1	528,009	-1.4
1955[g]	444,193	-2.6	469,816	-3.2	452,721	2.3	557,740	1.5	408,705	-0.7	521,878	-1.2
1956[h]	456,768	2.8	490,174	4.3	453,759	0.2	566,471	1.6	396,456	-3.0	496,798	-4.8
1957[i]	471,203	3.2	505,806	3.2	468,167	3.2	579,068	2.2	397,832	0.3	493,949	-0.6
1958[j]	456,117	-3.2	494,506	-2.2	463,469	-1.0	575,276	-0.7	391,295	-1.6	486,113	-1.6
1959[k]	498,912	9.4	521,656	5.5	468,540	1.1	583,614	1.4	385,908	-1.4	472,366	-2.8

Sources:

a. *Editor & Publisher International Yearbook, 1950* (New York: Editor & Publisher, 1950), 72.

b. *Editor & Publisher International Yearbook, 1951* (New York: Editor & Publisher, 1951), 72.

c. *Editor & Publisher International Yearbook, 1952* (New York: Editor & Publisher, 1952), 70.

d. *Editor & Publisher International Yearbook, 1953* (New York: Editor & Publisher, 1953), 76.

e. *Editor & Publisher International Yearbook, 1954* (New York: Editor & Publisher, 1954), 80, 82.

f. *Editor & Publisher International Yearbook, 1955* (New York: Editor & Publisher, 1955), 82.

g. *Editor & Publisher International Yearbook, 1956* (New York: Editor & Publisher, 1956), 82.

h. *Editor & Publisher International Yearbook, 1957* (New York: Editor & Publisher, 1957), 84, 86.

i. *Editor & Publisher International Yearbook, 1958* (New York: Editor & Publisher, 1958), 82.

j. *Editor & Publisher International Yearbook, 1959* (New York: Editor & Publisher, 1959), 92, 94.

k. *Editor & Publisher International Yearbook, 1960* (New York: Editor & Publisher, 1960), 136

Table 20. Favorite Detroit television channel, 1962

Station	%
WWJ-TV	32
WJBK-TV	26
WXYZ-TV	23
CKLW-TV	3
All	1
None	4
Don't know/No response	11

Source: McHugh and Hoffman, Inc., "A Study of Viewer Attitudes toward Television in Detroit," 1962, box 103808, 103, McHugh and Hoffman files, Bentley Historical Library, University of Michigan, Ann Arbor.

Table 21. 11 p.m. news ratings, Monday–Friday, March 1965

Station	Rating	Audience
WWJ-TV	21	2,829,000
WJBK-TV	14	1,652,000
WXYZ-TV	5	620,000

Source: American Research Bureau, Detroit Television Audience, March 1965, E, Hargrett Rare Book and Manuscript Library, University of Georgia, Athens.

Table 22. WJBK-TV local newscasts, 1960–69

Date	Time slot	Minutes	Total
December 19, 1960[a]	6:25 p.m.	:15	
	6:45 p.m.	:15	
	11 p.m.	:15	45 minutes
January 12, 1961[b]	6:25 p.m.	:15	
	6:45 p.m.	:15	
	11 p.m.	:15	45 minutes
March 29, 1962[c]	11:55 a.m.	:05	
	6:30 p.m.	:10	
	11 p.m.	:15	30 minutes
September 19, 1963[d]	7 a.m.	:10	
	12:25 p.m.	:05	
	3:25 p.m.	:05	
	6 p.m.	:15	
	11 p.m.	:15	50 minutes
June 18, 1964[e]	7 a.m.	:10	
	12:25 p.m.	:05	
	3:25 p.m.	:05	
	6 p.m.	:15	
	11 p.m.	:15	50 minutes
July 1, 1965[f]	6:50 a.m.	:10	
	12:25 p.m.	:05	
	3:25 p.m.	:05	
	6 p.m.	:15	
	11 p.m.	:15	50 minutes
July 28, 1966[g]	6:20 a.m.	:05	
	6:55 a.m.	:05	
	12 p.m.	:30	
	1:25 p.m.	:05	
	3:25 p.m.	:05	
	6 p.m.	:30	
	11 p.m.	:30	110 minutes
October 16, 1967[h]	6:20 a.m.	:10	
	12 p.m.	:25	
	1:25 p.m.	:05	
	6 p.m.	:30	
	11 p.m.	:30	100 minutes

Table 22. WJBK-TV local newscasts, 1960–69 *(continued)*

Date	Time slot	Minutes	Total
December 19, 1968[i]	5:50 a.m.	:10	
	12 p.m.	:25	
	1:25 p.m.	:05	
	4:25 p.m.	:05	
	6 p.m.	:30	
	11 p.m.	:30	105 minutes
September 22, 1969[j]	7:30 a.m.	:30	
	12 p.m.	:25	
	2:25 p.m.	:05	
	6 p.m.	:30	
	11 p.m.	:30	120 minutes

Sources:
a. *Detroit Free Press Weekly TV Magazine*, December 18–24, 1960, 7D–8D.
b. *Detroit Free Press Weekly TV Magazine*, January 8–14, 1961, 17D–18D.
c. *Detroit News TV Magazine*, March 25–31, 1962, 51, 53, 55–56.
d. *Detroit News TV Magazine*, September 15–21, 1963, 60, 61, 62–66.
e. *Detroit News TV Magazine*, June 14–20, 1964, 63, 64, 65, 66–69.
f. *Detroit News TV Magazine*, June 27–July 3, 1965, 63, 64, 65–69.
g. *TV Guide*, July 23–29, 1966, A62, A63, A64, A65–A69.
h. *TV Guide*, October 14–20, 1967, A60, A62, A63, A64, A67.
i. *TV Guide*, December 14–20, 1968, A58, A59, A60, A61, A62, A66.
j. *Detroit News TV Magazine*, September 21–27, 1969, 44–56.

Table 23. WWJ-TV local newscasts, 1960–69

Date	Time slot	Minutes	Total
December 19, 1960[a]	6:30 p.m.	:10	
	6:45 p.m.	:15	
	11 p.m.	:15	40 minutes
January 12, 1961[b]	1 p.m.	:05	
	6:30 p.m.	:10	
	6:45 p.m.	:15	
	11 p.m.	:15	45 minutes
March 29, 1962[c]	8:25 a.m.	:05	
	6:30 p.m.	:10	
	11 p.m.	:15	30 minutes
September 19, 1963[d]	8:25 a.m.	:05	
	6 p.m.	:15	
	11 p.m.	:15	35 minutes
June 18, 1964[e]	8:25 a.m.	:05	
	6 p.m.	:15	
	11 p.m.	:15	35 minutes
July 1, 1965[f]	7:25 a.m.	:05	
	8:25 a.m.	:05	
	9:55 a.m.	:05	
	6 p.m.	:15	
	11 p.m.	:15	45 minutes
July 28, 1966[g]	6:20 a.m.	:10	
	9:55 a.m.	:05	
	10:25 a.m.	:05	
	12:55 p.m.	:05	
	6 p.m.	:30	
	11 p.m.	:30	85 minutes
October 16, 1967[h]	10:25 a.m.	:05	
	12:55 p.m.	:05	
	6 p.m.	:05	
	11 p.m.	:30	
		:30	70 minutes
December 19, 1968[i]	10:25 a.m.	:05	
	12:25 p.m.	:05	
	6 p.m.	:30	
	11 p.m.	:30	70 minutes

Table 23. WWJ-TV local newscasts, 1960–69 *(continued)*

Date	Time slot	Minutes	Total
September 22, 1969[j]	7:25 a.m.	:05	
	12:30 p.m.	:05	
	6 p.m.	:05	
	7 p.m.	:30	
	11 p.m.	:30	125 minutes

Sources:
a. *Detroit Free Press Weekly TV Magazine*, December 18–24, 1960, 6D–8D.
b. *Detroit Free Press Weekly TV Magazine*, January 8–14, 1961, 17D–18D.
c. *Detroit News TV Magazine*, March 25–31, 1962, 50–53, 55.
d. *Detroit News TV Magazine*, September 15–21, 1963, 60, 63–66.
e. *Detroit News TV Magazine*, June 14–20, 1964, 63–66, 69.
f. *Detroit News TV Magazine*, June 27–July 3, 1965, 63, 64, 66–69.
g. *TV Guide*, July 23–29, 1966, A62. A64, A64, A65–69.
h. *TV Guide*, October 14–20, 1967, A27–A28, A29, A31, A36.
i. *TV Guide*, December 14–20, 1968, A59, A62, A66.
j. *Detroit News TV Magazine*, September 21–27, 1969, 44–56.

Table 24. WXYZ-TV local newscasts, 1960–69

Date	Time slot	Minutes	Total
December 19, 1960[a]	9:50 a.m.	:10	
	6:00 p.m.	:10	
	6:15 p.m.	:15	35 minutes
January 12, 1961[b]	9:50 a.m.	:10	
	6 p.m.	:10	
	6:15 p.m.	:15	35 minutes
March 29, 1962[c]	10:25 a.m.	:05	
	6:30 p.m.	:15	
	11:12 p.m.	:18	38 minutes
September 19, 1963[d]	10:15 a.m.	:15	
	2:55 p.m.	:05	
	6:30 p.m.	:15	
	11:10 p.m.	:10	45 minutes
June 18, 1964[e]	2:20 p.m.	:10	
	2:55 p.m.	:05	
	6:30 p.m.	:30	
	11 p.m.	:30	75 minutes
July 1, 1965[f]	6:30 p.m.	:30	
	11 p.m.	:15	45 minutes
July 28, 1966[g]	8:25 a.m.	:05	
	5 p.m.	:45	
	11 p.m.	:30	80 minutes
October 16, 1967[h]	2:55 p.m.	:05	
	4:30 p.m.	:60	
	11 p.m.	:30	95 minutes
December 19, 1968[i]	6 p.m.	:60	
	11 p.m.	:30	90 minutes
September 22, 1969[j]	6 p.m.	:60	
	11 p.m.	:30	90 minutes

Sources:
a. *Detroit Free Press Weekly TV Magazine*, December 18–24, 1960, 6D–7D.
b. *Detroit Free Press Weekly TV Magazine*, January 8–14, 1961, 15D–17D.
c. *Detroit News TV Magazine*, March 25–31, 1962, 50, 53, 55.
d. *Detroit News TV Magazine*, September 15–21, 1963, 60, 62, 63–66.
e. *Detroit News TV Magazine*, June 14–20, 1964, 65, 66–69.
f. *Detroit News TV Magazine*, June 27–July 3, 1965, 66–69.
g. *TV Guide*, July 23–29, 1966, A62–A65, A69.
h. *TV Guide*, October 14–20, 1967, A27–A29, A30, A36.
i. *TV Guide*, December 14–20, 1968, A62, A66.
j. *Detroit News TV Magazine*, September 21–27, 1969, 44–56.

Table 25. Detroit radio revenue, 1960–69

Year	Number of stations	Revenue	% change	Expenses	% change	Net income	% change
1960	11	$10,828,933	5.2	$7,751,588	7.1	$3,077,345	0.6
1961	11	$9,555,712	-11.8	$7,510,658	-3.1	$2,045,054	-33.5
1962	11	$10,275,672	7.5	$7,742,138	3.1	$2,533,534	23.9
1963	12	$10,549,469	2.7	$8,371,596	8.1	$2,177,873	-14.0
1964	12	$12,974,726	23.0	$9,431,831	12.7	$3,542,895	62.7
1965	12	$13,786,007	6.3	$10,962,114	16.2	$2,823,893	-20.3
1966	13	$15,376,429	11.5	$11,779,307	7.5	$3,597,122	27.4
1967	13	$15,269,854	-0.7	$12,339,110	4.8	$2,930,744	-18.5
1968	12	$18,795,413	23.1	$13,147,556	6.6	$5,647,857	92.7
1969	12	$17,862,890	-5.0	$13,393,449	1.9	$4,469,441	-20.9

Source: FCC, "Broadcast Revenues, Expenses and Income (Before Federal Income Tax) of the Radio Broadcast Service," available at the Library of American Broadcasting, University of Maryland, College Park.

Table 26. Detroit television broadcast revenue, 1960–69

Year	Revenue	% change	Expenses	% change	Net income	% change
1960	$18,138,798	4.0	$9,912,697	1.4	$8,226,101	7.2
1961	$17,986,762	-0.8	$10,137,889	2.3	$7,848,873	-4.6
1962	$20,232,778	12.5	$10,969,223	8.2	$9,263,555	18.0
1963	$20,956,377	3.6	$11,176,720	1.9	$9,779,657	5.6
1964	$25,095,850	19.8	$13,041,828	16.7	$12,054,022	23.3
1965	$27,662,959	10.2	$15,271,441	17.1	$12,391,518	2.8
1966	$29,974,441	8.4	$17,168,441	12.4	$12,806,000	3.3
1967	$31,175,422	4.0	$18,425,541	7.3	$12,749,881	-.4
1968	$38,035,032	22.0	$21,455,120	16.4	$16,579,912	30.0
1969	$42,918,522	12.8	$23,771,940	10.8	$19,146,582	15.5

Source: FCC, "Broadcast Revenues, Expenses and Income (Before Federal Income Tax) of the Radio Broadcast Service," available at the Library of American Broadcasting, University of Maryland, College Park.

Table 27. Detroit newspaper circulation, 1961–69

Year	Detroit Free Press daily	% change	Detroit Free Press Sunday	% change	Detroit News daily	% change	Detroit News Sunday	% change
1961[a]	550,000	10.2	600,014	15.0	723,578	54.4	914,523	56.7
1962[b]	509,256	-7.4	561,432	-6.4	702,897	-2.9	913,648	-0.1
1963[c]	512,259	0.6	567,017	1.0	701,935	-0.1	926,200	1.4
1964[d]	521,257	1.8	577,640	1.9	707,418	0.8	942,193	1.7
1965[e]	509,410	-2.3	555,779	-3.8	682,834	-3.5	917,360	-2.6
1966[f]	537,203	5.5	580,412	4.4	684,705	0.3	684,705	-25.4
1967[g]	590,546	9.9	631,175	8.7	702,321	2.6	947,155	38.3
1968[h]	530,264	-10.2	578,254	-8.4	592,616	-15.6	827,086	-12.7
1969[i]	562,005	6.0	611,040	5.7	609,213	2.8	825,423	-0.2

Sources:

a. *Editor & Publisher International Yearbook, 1962* (New York: Editor & Publisher, 1962), 132.
b. *Editor & Publisher International Yearbook, 1963* (New York: Editor & Publisher, 1963), 129.
c. *Editor & Publisher International Yearbook, 1964* (New York: Editor & Publisher, 1964), 150.
d. *Editor & Publisher International Yearbook, 1965* (New York: Editor & Publisher, 1965), 151.
e. *Editor & Publisher International Yearbook, 1966* (New York: Editor & Publisher, 1966), 134.
f. *Editor & Publisher International Yearbook, 1967* (New York: Editor & Publisher, 1967), 135.
g. *Editor & Publisher International Yearbook, 1968* (New York: Editor & Publisher, 1968), 131, 134.
h. *Editor & Publisher International Yearbook, 1969* (New York: Editor & Publisher, 1969), 137.
i. *Editor & Publisher International Yearbook, 1970* (New York: Editor & Publisher, 1970), 138.

Table 28. 11 p.m.–11:15 p.m. news ratings, Monday–Friday, July 6–August 2, 1967

Station	Rating	Households
WWJ-TV	18	249,500
WJBK-TV	17	224,400
WXYZ-TV	14	179,600

Source: American Research Bureau, Detroit Television Market, July 1967, D, Hargrett Rare Book and Manuscript Library, University of Georgia, Athens.

Table 29. Network and owned-station profits, 1959–77

Year	Network profits (millions)	Owned-station profits (millions)
1959	$32.0	$55.9
1960	$33.6	$61.6
1961	$24.7	$62.3
1962	$36.7	$74.7
1963	$56.4	$79.8
1964	$60.2	$96.3
1965	$59.4	$102.2
1966	$78.7	$108.1
1967	$55.8	$104.3
1968	$56.4	$122.4
1969	$92.7	$133.4
1970	$50.1	$117.3
1971	$53.7	$91.2
1972	$110.9	$102.5
1973	$184.8	$102.8
1974	$225.1	$105.7
1975	$208.5	$105.7
1976	$295.6	$159.0
1977	$406.1	$149.3

Source: Cobbett S. Steinberg, *TV Facts* (New York: Facts on File, 1980), 492.

Table 30. ABC revenue and net income, 1970–79

Year	Revenue from continuing operations (thousands)	% change	Earnings from continuing operations (thousands)	% change
1970	$702,430	3.3	$14,089	-9.3
1971	$713,437	1.6	$13,351	-5.2
1972	$819,498	14.9	$33,818	153.3
1973	$880,505	7.4	$45,470	34.5
1974	$986,040	12.0	$49,945	9.8
1975	$1,064,648	8.0	$17,096	-65.8
1976	$1,269,795	19.3	$71,747	319.7
1977	$1,535,667	20.9	$106,961	49.1
1978	$1,783,985	16.2	$127,510	19.2
1979	$2,053,570	15.1	$159,310	24.9

Sources: ABC Annual Reports, 1973, 1976, and 1980; available at ProQuest Historical Annual Reports, http://www.proquest.com/products_pq/descriptions/pq_hist_annual_repts.shtml.

Table 31. Storer Broadcasting revenue and net income, 1974–79

Year	Revenue (thousands)	% change	Net income (thousands)	% change	Margin (%)
1974	$69,954		$21,506		30.7
1975	$75,413	7.8	$20,085	-6.6	26.6
1976	$94,377	25.1	$29,659	47.7	31.4
1977	$99,278	5.2	$26,659	-10.1	26.9
1978	$118,488	19.3	$35,698	33.9	30.1
1979	$130,083	9.8	$40,274	12.8	31.0

Sources: Storer Annual Reports, 1974–79; available at ProQuest Historical Annual Reports, http://www.proquest.com/products_pq/descriptions/pq_hist_annual_repts.shtml.

Table 32. 11 p.m. news ratings, Monday–Friday, October 1967

Station	Rating	Household share
WWJ-TV	14	37
WJBK-TV	15	38
WXYZ-TV	11	28

Source: American Research Bureau, Detroit Television Audience, September 27, 1967–October 24, 1967, G, Hargrett Rare Book and Manuscript Library, University of Georgia, Athens.

Table 33. 11 p.m. news rating among metropolitan black households, November 1976

Station	Rating	Household share
WWJ-TV	9	16
WJBK-TV	30	51
WXYZ-TV	19	32

Source: Arbitron Survey of Black Households, Metropolitan Detroit, November 1976, 15.

Table 34. 11 p.m. news ratings/shares, 1974–78

Year	WWJ-TV	WJBK-TV	WXYZ-TV
1974[a]	13/26	17/34	18/36
1975[b]	12/24	12/26	22/46
1976[c]	10/22	14/30	19/40
1977[d]	10/21	16/33	20/41
1978[e]	13/25	16/31	19/37

Sources: Arbitron Estimates in the Arbitron Market of Detroit, in author's possession.
a. February 6–March 5, 1974, 10.
b. February 5–March 4, 1975, 10.
c. February 4–March 2, 1976, 10.
d. February 2–March 1, 1977, 10.
e. February 1–28, 1978, 10.

Table 35. Viewer drop-off, 1974–1978

Station and year	10:30 p.m. market share	11 p.m. market share	Drop-in market points	% drop
WJBK-TV				
1974[a]	19	17	-2	-10.5
1975[b]	20	12	-8	-40.0
1976[c]	19	14	-5	-26.3
1977[d]	15	16	1	6.7
1978[e]	20	16	-4	-20.0
WXYZ-TV				
1974[a]	22	18	-4	-18.0
1975[b]	19	22	3	15.8
1976[c]	26	19	-7	-26.9
1977[d]	28	20	-8	-28.6
1978[e]	23	19	-4	-17.4
WWJ-TV				
1974[a]	20	13	-7	-35.0
1975[b]	21	12	-9	-42.9
1976[c]	16	10	-6	-37.5
1977[d]	16	10	-6	-37.5
1978[e]	20	13	-7	-35.0

Sources: Arbitron Estimates in the Arbitron Market of Detroit, in author's possession.
a. February 6–March 5, 1974, 10.
b. February 5–March 4, 1975, 10.
c. February 4–March 2, 1976, 10.
d. February 2–March 1, 1977, 10.
e. February 1–28, 1978, 10.

Table 36. 11 p.m. news ratings/shares, 1982–87

Year	WJBK-TV	WDIV-TV	WXYZ-TV
1982[a]	11/23	11/23	18/38
1983[b]	10/19	12/23	22/43
1984[c]	15/26	13/24	17/31
1985[d]	12/23	13/25	16/30
1986[e]	13/24	16/29	13/24
1987[f]	11/21	15/29	13/25

Sources: Arbitron Estimates in the Arbitron Market of Detroit, in author's possession.
a. February 3–March 2, 1982, DPS3.
b. February 2–March 1, 1983, DPS3.
c. February 1–28, 1984, DPS5.
d. January 30–February 26, 1985, 10.
e. January 29–February 25, 1986, 10.
f. February 4–March 3, 1987, 5.

Table 37. Favorite TV station by class, 1973 (with percent change from 1971)

Station	Upper-middle	Lower-middle	Upper-lower	Lower-lower
WJBK-TV	26% (+4%)	23% (-3%)	27% (-3%)	30% (-2%)
WWJ-TV	20% (+2%)	31% (+11%)	24% (+5%)	17% (+5%)
WXYZ-TV	29% (+14%)	29% (+10%)	37% (+11%)	28% (+11%)
Other/No choice	25% (-20%)	17% (-18%)	12% (-17%)	25% (-16%)

Source: McHugh and Hoffman, Inc., "Essential Findings and Recommendations for WJBK-TV," June 8, 1973, 3, McHugh and Hoffman files, Bentley Historical Library, University of Michigan, Ann Arbor.

Table 38. Favorite newscaster, 1973 (compared with 1971)

Newscaster	1973	1971
Bill Bonds	29%	16%
Jac Le Goff	21%	21%
John Kelly	10%	8%
Dean Miller	4%	—

Source: McHugh and Hoffman, Inc., "Essential Findings and Recommendations for WJBK-TV," June 8, 1973, 11, McHugh and Hoffman files, Bentley Historical Library, University of Michigan, Ann Arbor.

Table 39. WJBK-TV news ratings, 1976–79

Year	6 p.m. newscast	11 p.m. newscast
1976	17[a]	14[b]
1977	16[c]	16[d]
1978	13[e]	16[f]
1979	10[g]	11[h]

Sources: Arbitron Esimates in the Arbitron Markets of Detroit, in author's possession.
a. February 4–March 2, 1976, 16.
b. February 4–March 2, 1976, 10.
c. February 2–March 1, 1977, 16.
d. February 2–March 1, 1977, 10.
e. February 1–28, 1978, 16.
f. February 1–28, 1978, 10.
g. January 31–February 27, 1979, 16.
h. January 31–February 27, 1979.

Table 40. Favorite television station, February 1979

Station	%
WXYZ-TV (Channel 7)	34
WJBK-TV (Channel 2)	16
WDIV-TV (Channel 4)	13
WKBD-TV (Channel 50)	10
WTVS-TV (Channel 56)	3
Other	1
No preference	34

Source: Peter S. Hoffman, "Essential Findings and Recommendations—Detroit Market Study," Winter 1979, box 103809, 2, McHugh and Hoffman files, Bentley Historical Library, University of Michigan, Ann Arbor.

Table 41. Television news content (in percentages), December 2–6, 1996, through January 13–17, 1997

Subject	WJBK-TV	WDIV-TV	WXYZ-TV	WKBD-TV
Crime	24	37	34	28
Disaster	13	17	15	12
Human interest	19	12	13	8
Politics/Government	1	2	10	7
Weather news	7	8	8	9
Business	8	1	0	3
Consumer	10	7	6	15
Health	10	11	8	9
Celebrity	5	4	2	3
Science	0	1	1	2
Religion	1	0	2	0
Race	0	0	0	2
International	0	1	1	0
Poverty	1	0	0	1
Education	0	0	0	0
Comment	2	0	0	0

Source: Tim Kiska, "Violence," *Detroit News*, February 16, 1997, 8A.

Notes

INTRODUCTION

1. Author's interview with Armand Gebert, January 9, 2007. Unless otherwise noted by phrase "notes in author's possession," all interviews are taped and in author's possession.

2. The author was employed as an editorial assistant at the *Detroit Free Press* beginning September 25, 1970. He left the newspaper March 1, 1987.

3. Census by William McGraw, April 2, 2007. (Bill went around and counted the number of sets in the *Free Press* newsroom.) The *Detroit News* has thirty television sets in its offices (census by Susan Whitall, May 8, 2008).

4. Mike Wendland, "Free Press, Local 4 Join News Forces, Plan Michigan Polling," *Detroit Free Press*, April 27, 2006.

5. A. J. Wood Research Corporation, "A Study of Evening News Programs in Detroit," March 1965, 16, McHugh and Hoffman files, Bentley Historical Library, University of Michigan, Ann Arbor.

6. According to the Arbitron ratings service, 5 percent of Detroit area households had cable television in 1982. The number increased to 10 percent in 1983 and 20 percent in 1984. As of 2008, the number stands at two-thirds.

7. Amy Mitchell, associate director of the Project for Excellence in Journalism, speech given at the Forum on Media Ownership, Columbia University, January 16, 2003.

8. Radio Television News Directors Foundation's 2006 Future of News Survey, available at http://www.rtnda.org/resources/future/section2.pdf.

9. Matthew R. Kerbel, *If It Bleeds, It Leads: An Anatomy of Television News* (Boulder, CO: Westview, 2000), 131.

10. Press release, "Survey Examines Excesses and Improvements in Local TV Newscasts across the U.S.," August 4, 1998, http://www.bigmedia.org/texts5.html (accessed January 9, 2007).

11. Craig Allen, *News Is People: The Rise of Local TV News and the Fall of News from New York* (Ames: Iowa State University Press, 2001).

12. Dick Osgood, *W*Y*X*I*E Wonderland: An Unauthorized 50-Year Diary of WXYZ Detroit* (Bowling Green, OH: Bowling Green University Popular Press, 1981).

13. Osgood spells Grosse Pointe "Grosse Point" on p. 169; refers to *Wixie's Wonderland*, a television show, as *Wyxie Wonderland* on p. 314; calls actress Mary Martin "Marty" Martin on p. 330; and *Detroit Free Press* television critic Bettelou Peterson is "Bette Lou" on pp. 345 and 389.

14. John Kelly and Marilyn Turner, *Good Morning Detroit: The*

Kelly & Co. Story (Chicago: Contemporary, 1986).

15. Gordon Castelnero, *TV Land—Detroit* (Ann Arbor: University of Michigan Press, 2006).

16. Don F. DeGroot, *Living on Air* (N.p.: Oakmore, 1978).

17. Tim Kiska, "Unintended Consequences: A History of Detroit Television News" (PhD diss., Wayne State University, 2003); Tim Kiska, *From Soupy to Nuts: A History of Detroit Television* (Royal Oak, MI: Momentum, 2005).

CHAPTER 1

1. Reuven Frank, *Out of Thin Air* (New York: Simon & Schuster, 1991), back dust jacket.

2. Detroit News, *WWJ—The Detroit News* (Detroit: Evening News Association, 1922), 7.

3. William S. Paley, *As It Happened: A Memoir* (Garden City, NY: Doubleday, 1979), 118.

4. Detroit News, *WWJ*, 25, 33, 21, 19.

5. Ibid., 20.

6. George H. Douglas, *The Early Days of Radio Broadcasting* (Jefferson, NC: McFarland, 1987), 98.

7. Erik Barnouw, *A Tower in Babel: A History of Broadcasting in the United States* (New York: Oxford University Press, 1966), 1:138.

8. Al Weeks, "Tribute to a Small Town Guy," *Detroit News*, August 11, 1940.

9. Curtis C. Bradner, editorial, *Detroit Times*, August 8, 1940.

10. Ibid.

11. Harry Bannister, *The Education of a Broadcaster* (New York: Simon & Schuster, 1965), 126.

12. Ibid.

13. "Last Tribute Paid to Brad," *Detroit News*, August 9, 1940.

14. Fran Harris, "Instant Newscaster" (unpublished memoir in author's possession), 4.

15. "Impartiality Marked Political News Coverage," *Editor & Publisher*, November 10, 1928, 5.

16. Russell J. Hammargren, "The Origin of Press-Radio Conflict," *Journalism Quarterly* 15 (1938): 93.

17. Ralph D. Casey, *Freedom of the Press*, Newspaper Radio Committee pamphlet, Hedges Collection, box 21, Newspaper Ownership of Stations, (A, E), 18, University of Maryland Library of American Broadcasting, College Park.

18. Ibid.

19. Ibid.

20. Jean Folkerts and Dwight L. Teeter Jr., *Voices of a Nation*, 3rd ed. (Boston: Allyn & Bacon, 1998), 389.

21. Casey, *Freedom of the Press*, 15.

22. Ibid., 33.

23. *Broadcasting*, February 1, 1938, 19.

24. George E. Lott Jr., "The Press-Radio War of the 1930s," *Journal of Broadcasting* 14, no. 3 (1970): 279.

25. "Buckley's Words Revived," *New York Times*, March 21, 1931, 3.

26. "Killing of Buckley Arouses Detroit; Hint of Racketeer," *New York Times*, July 24, 1930, 1.

27. Paley, *As It Happened*, 118.

28. Ibid., 120.

29. Obituary of Edward Klauber, *New York Times*, September 24, 1954, 23.

30. United Press, "Paul White Dies; Radio Newsman," *New York Times*, July 10, 1955, 72.

31. A. M. Sperber, *Murrow: His Life and Times* (New York: Freundlich, 1986), 99.

32. David Holbrook Culbert, *News for Everyman* (Westport, CT: Greenwood, 1976), 20.

33. Raymond Swing, *Good Evening! A Professional Memoir by Raymond Swing* (Harcourt, Brace & World, 1964), 189.

34. H.v. [Hans] Kaltenborn, *Fifty Fabulous Years, 1900–1950: A Personal Review* (New York: Putnam, 1950), 208.

35. William L. Shirer, *The Nightmare Years: 1930–1940* (New York: Bantam, 1985), 280, 281.

36. Author's telephone interview with James F. Clark, June 26, 2003.

37. Harris, "Instant Newscaster," 7.

38. Clark, interview.

39. Associated Press, "F.C.C. Asked to Bar 3 Radio Stations," *New York Times*, May 16, 1951, 52.

40. Associated Press, "G. A. Richards, Owner of 3 Radio Stations," *New York Times*, May 28, 1951, 19.

41. United Press, "F.C.C. Shifts Hearings," *New York Times*, October 20, 1950, 30.

42. *Detroit Times*, June 2, 1957; also Guy Nunn biographical file, Archives of Labor and Urban Affairs, Walter P. Reuther Library, Detroit.

43. Paul W. White, *News on the Air* (New York: Harcourt, Brace, 1947), 2.

44. Ibid.

45. Ibid., 4.

46. Sally Bedell Smith, *In All His Glory* (New York: Simon & Schuster, 1990), 166.

CHAPTER 2

1. Columbia Broadcasting System, *Television News Reporting* (New York: McGraw-Hill, 1958), 2.

2. Federal Communications Commission [hereafter FCC], *Twelfth Report* (Washington, DC: Government Printing Office [hereafter GPO], 1946), 9, 10.

3. FCC, *Thirteenth Report* (Washington, DC: GPO, 1947), 29.

4. FCC, *Fourteenth Report* (Washington, DC: GPO, 1948), 26, 27.

5. Fran Harris, "Instant Newscaster" (unpublished memoir in author's possession), 72.

6. William W. Lutz, *The News of Detroit* (Boston: Little, Brown, 1973), 90.

7. *TV Facts* (New York: Facts on File, 1980), 496.

8. "Television Comes to Town," *Detroit News*, October 24, 1946, 30.

9. "Congratulations to WWDT," *Detroit News*, October 24, 1946, 19.

10. "Wings Lose 3rd," *Detroit News*, October 24, 1946, 49.

11. "Television Sets Stir Enthusiasm," *New York Times*, October 12, 1946.

12. Lawrence E. Davies, "Television Ready, RCA Experts Say," *New York Times*, August 31, 1946.

13. "Capital Exercises Are Telecast Here," *New York Times*, February 13, 1946.

14. *Broadcasting*, October 7, 1946, 13.

15. Ibid., 62.

16. Ibid., 50.

17. Jack Gould, "Television in Focus," *New York Times*, May 26, 1946.

18. "Television Comes to City, Hustles Out to Ball Game," *Detroit News*, October 4, 1947, 4.

19. Frank Marx, "Television Story Began in 1873," *Detroit Free Press*, October 8, 1948, 22, 23.

20. Bureau of Labor Statistics, Consumer Price Index Inflation Calculator, http://data.bls.gov/cgi-bin/cipac.pl (accessed April 23, 2007).

21. *Broadcasting*, November 29, 1948, 10.

22. "George Booth, 84, Detroit Publisher," *New York Times*, April 12, 1949.

23. Obituary of William Scripps, *New York Times*, June 13, 1952.

24. Lutz, *News of Detroit*, 90.

25. *Broadcasting*, October 7, 1946, 98.

26. Ibid.

27. *Broadcasting*, November 8, 1948, 15, 23.

28. "ABC Files Request to Issue New Stock," *New York Times*, May 24, 1946.

29. Leonard Goldenson, *Beating the Odds* (New York: Charles Scribner's Sons, 1991), 99.

30. *Broadcasting*, February 3, 1947, 16.

31. *Broadcasting*, January 20, 1947, 21.

32. John Floyd Wellman, "Storer Broadcasting Company—Its History, Organization and Operation" (PhD diss., University of Michigan, 1973), 15.

33. Ibid., 57.

34. Obituary of J. Harold Ryan, *New York Times*, June 7, 1961.

35. "Fly Named in Sale of Florida Station," *New York Times*, September 6, 1944.

36. Dick Osgood, *W*Y*X*I*E Wonderland: An Unauthorized 50-Year Diary of WXYZ Detroit* (Bowling Green, OH: Bowling Green University Popular Press, 1981), 263.

37. *Detroit Free Press*, October 8, 1948, 32.

38. *Broadcasting*, November 1, 1948, 85.

39. Tim Kiska, *From Soupy to Nuts: A History of Detroit Television* (Royal Oak, MI: Momentum, 2005), vii, viii.

40. Ibid., 190–91.

41. Chris Kucharski, "Morton Zieve: Adman Also Directed for TV and Stage," *Detroit Free Press*, August 10, 2005, 5B.

42. *TV Today*, July 15–21, 1950, 12.

43. Author's telephone interview with James F. Clark, June 25, 2003.

44. Author's interview with Sid Siegal, April 12, 2007.

45. Ibid.

46. Author's interview with Sonny Eliot, July 30, 2003.

47. Author's interview with Jac Le Goff, May 12, 2003.

48. *Detroit News*, October 5, 1986, 15.

49. David Brinkley, *13 Presidents, 4 Wars, 22 Political Conventions, 1 Moon Landing, 3 Assassinations, 2,000 Weeks of News and Other Stuff on Television and 18 Years of Growing Up in North Carolina* (New York: Alfred A. Knopf, 1995), 105.

50. Author's interview with Dave Diles, June 23, 2003.

51. Osgood, *W*Y*X*I*E Wonderland*, 373.

52. *TV Channel: The Detroit Free Press Weekly TV Magazine*, January 8–14, 1961, 8D, 11D, 14D, 18D, 21D.

53. Ron Garay, "Television and the 1951 Senate Crime Committee Hearings," *Journal of Broadcasting* 22, no. 4 (1978): 473.

54. "Crime Hearings, Commercial Shows Cancelled," *Broadcasting/Telecasting*, February 26, 1951, 56.

55. Clark, interview, May 11, 2000.

56. Ibid.

57. Ibid.

58. Author's interview with Bill Bonds, May 21, 2003 (notes in author's possession).

59. Author's interview with Carl Cederberg, April 21, 2001 (notes in author's possession).

60. Clark, interview, June 23, 2003.

61. Ibid.; Paul Williams biographical file, Detroit News Library, Detroit.

62. Cederberg, interview, May 12, 2002.

63. Bonds, interview, May 19, 2003.

64. Clark, interview, June 23, 2003.

65. Tim Kiska, "Ven Marshall Succumbs: TV Reporter Covered Top Stories for 31 Years," *Detroit News*, February 2, 1989, B1.

66. Author's interview with Ken Hissong, June 27, 2003 (notes in author's possession).

67. Eliot, interview, June 27, 2003.

68. Clark, interview, June 26, 2003.

69. Author's interview with Dwayne X. Riley, April 30, 2003.

70. E. L. Shurmur testimonial dinner program (in author's possession).

71. Berl Falbaum, *The Anchor, Leo & Friends* (Eugene, OR: JDW, 1978), 101.

72. Everett W. Phelps biographical file, Archives of Labor and Urban Affairs, Walter P. Reuther Library, Detroit.

73. Frank Judge, "Le Goff Fired by WJBK, Sticks to Stand on Payola," *Detroit News*, November 20, 1959, 1A, 4A.

74. Tim Brooks and Earle Marsh, *The Complete Directory to Prime Time Network and Cable TV Shows, 1946–Present* (New York: Ballantine, 1995), xiii.

75. Ibid., 1258.

76. Ibid., xv.

77. Ibid., 19 (October 26, 1948).

78. Ibid., 15 (June 15, 1945).

79. The Lady of Charm, aka Edythe Fern Melrose, *The Charm Kitchen Cookbook (Cook for a Man So He Loves It, Then He'll Love the Cook!)* (Detroit: House O'Charm, 1948), 5.

80. Osgood, *W*Y*X*I*E Wonderland*, 352.

81. Bureau of Labor Statistics, Inflation Calculator.

82. Eliot, interview, May 24, 2003.

83. Ibid.

84. Ibid.

85. Author's interview with Jack Casey, May 19, 2003.

86. FCC, *Fifteenth Report* (Washington, DC: GPO, 1949), 54.

87. Harry Bannister, *The Education of a Broadcaster* (New York: Simon & Schuster, 1965), 203.

88. FCC, *Sixteenth Report* (Washington, DC: GPO, 1950), 123.

89. *Journalism History* (Winter 1995): 164.

90. Arthur Unger, "Frank Stanton: Born to Indispensability," *Television Quarterly* 27, no. 1 (1994): 2.

91. Quincy Howe, "The Rise and Fall of the Radio Commentator," *Saturday Review*, October 26, 1957, 15, 38.

92. American Society of Newspaper Editors, "Problems of Journalism: Proceedings of the Convention of the American Society of Newspaper Editors" (1951), 146, 152, Hatcher Graduate Library,

University of Michigan, Ann Arbor.

93. Ibid., 158.

94. American Society of Newspaper Editors, "Problems of Journalism, Proceedings of the Convention of the American Society of Newspaper Editors" (1952), 250, 261, 259, Hatcher Graduate Library, University of Michigan, Ann Arbor.

CHAPTER 3

1. Richard S. Salant, *Salant, CBS, and the Battle for the Soul of Broadcast Journalism*, ed. Susan Buzenberg and Bill Buzenberg (Boulder, CO: Westview, 1999), 41, 43.

2. Ibid., 43.

3. Ibid., 41.

4. Walter Cronkite, *A Reporter's Life* (New York: Alfred A. Knopf), 246.

5. Jack Gould, "TV: 2 Networks Add Emphasis on Current Events," *New York Times*, September 3, 1963.

6. John P. Shanley, "Cronkite—Experienced Newsman on the Air," *New York Times*, May 12, 1963.

7. Salant, *Salant, CBS and the Battle for the Soul of Broadcast Journalism*, 45, 46.

8. Ibid., 46–47.

9. Reuven Frank, *Out of Thin Air* (New York: Simon & Schuster, 1991), 133.

10. Tim Brooks and Earle Marsh, *The Complete Directory to Prime Time Network and Cable TV Shows, 1946–Present* (New York: Ballantine, 1995), 182.

11. "KNXT Plans 1½ Hours of News Night," *Los Angeles Times*, July 4, 1963.

12. William J. Hampton, *The First 80 Years: An Informal History of the Campbell-Ewald Company* (Warren, MI: Lintas-Campbell-Ewald, 1991), 76.

13. W. Lloyd Warner and Paul S. Lunt, *The Social Life of a Modern Community* (New Haven: Yale University Press, 1941), 26.

14. Social Research, Inc., "Television in the Greater Detroit Area, Late Winter," 1968, study 210/61, 9, McHugh and Hoffman files, Bentley Historical Library, University of Michigan, Ann Arbor.

15. Ibid., 9–11.

16. Social Research, Inc., "A Study of Viewer Attitudes toward Television in Detroit," July 1962, 88, McHugh and Hoffman files, Bentley Historical Library, University of Michigan, Ann Arbor.

17. Ibid., 125.

18. Ibid., 85.

19. Ibid.

20. Ibid, 132–33.

21. Social Research, Inc., "Viewer Attitudes toward Television in Detroit," 1963–64, box client #215, box 103808, 2, McHugh and Hoffman files, Bentley Historical Library, University of Michigan, Ann Arbor.

22. Author's interview with Henry Baskin, April 18, 2007.

23. Social Research, "Viewer Attitudes," 1963–64, 122–23.

24. Ibid., 2.

25. McHugh and Hoffman, Inc., "Essential Findings and Recommendations for WJBK-TV," March 15, 1966, 2, McHugh and Hoffman files, Bentley Historical Library, University of Michigan, Ann Arbor.

26. Author's telephone interview with James F. Clark, June 23, 2003.

27. James A. Brown and Ward L. Quaal, *Radio-Television-Cable Management*, 3rd ed. (Boston: McGraw-Hill, 1998), 236.

28. Leonard Goldenson, *Beating the Odds* (New York: Charles Scribner's Sons, 1991), 276.

29. Brooks and Marsh, *Complete Directory to Prime Time Network and Cable TV Shows*, 364.

30. A William Bluem, *Documentary in American Television* (New York: Hastings House, 1965), 233; Daniel Einstein, *Special Edition: A Guide to Network Television Documentary Series and Special News Reports, 1955–1979* (Metuchen, NJ: Scarecrow, 1987), 264.

31. Brooks and Marsh, *Complete Directory to Prime Time Network and Cable TV Shows*, 485.

32. John T. McQuiston, "James C. Hagerty, 71, Dies; Eisenhower Press Secretary," *New York Times*, April 13, 1981.

33. Author's interview with Peter Strand, May 12, 2003.

34. Author's interview with Dave Diles, May 10, 2003.

35. Dick Osgood, *W*Y*X*I*E Wonderland: An Unauthorized 50-Year Diary of WXYZ Detroit* (Bowling Green, OH: Bowling Green University Popular Press, 1981), 374.

36. *Detroit News TV Magazine*, March 25–31, 1962, 55.

37. Diles, interview.

38. Author's interview with Jim Herrington, June 20, 2003.

39. Author's interview with Barney Morris, November 22, 2001.

40. Author's interview with Bill Bonds, June 19, 2003.

41. Clark, interview, June 18, 2003.

42. Bonds, interview, May 21, 2003.

43. Ibid.

44. Herrington, interview.

CHAPTER 4

1. WJR newscast, 11 p.m., July 22, 1967, National Advisory Commission on Civil Disorders, series 41, box 9, Lyndon Baines Johnson Library, Austin, Texas (hereafter LBJ).

2. United Press International, "Birmingham Quells 200 Negro Youths," *New York Times*, July 23, 1967.

3. United Press International, "Fire and Explosions Strike Youngstown in Racial Violence," *New York Times*, July 23, 1967.

4. Thomas A. Johnson, "Negroes Disrupt Newark Parley," *New York Times*, July 23, 1967.

5. WJBK-TV studios at the time were located just north of the Fisher Building. The station moved its operations to Southfield, Michigan, in 1971. WTVS-TV (Channel 56) now occupies the former Channel 2 building.

6. WJR newscast, July 22, 1967, LBJ.

7. *Report of the National Advisory Commission on Civil Disorders* (New York: Bantam, 1968), 84.

8. Author's interview with Michael Kalush, April 14, 2003.

9. Author's interview with Thomas De Lisle, April 13, 2003.

10. Author's interview with Phil Nye, May 12, 2003.

11. Author's telephone interview with James F. Clark, June 26, 2003.

12. Author's interview with Marilyn Barnett, April 13, 2007.

13. Kalush, interview.

14. Author's interview with Don Haney, July 29, 2001.

15. Cavanagh and Robinson's connection would continue until, literally, the last moments of Cavanagh's life. Robinson later went to prison on federal charges resulting from a Florida land deal. Cavanagh died while visiting Robinson in a federal penitentiary in Kentucky. The two were planning Robinson's appeal.

16. Robinson to Cavanagh, Jerome P. Cavanagh Collection, box 362, folder 9, Wayne State University Archives of Labor and Urban Affairs, Detroit.

17. Jerome P. Cavanagh Collection, Wayne State University Archives of Labor and Urban Affairs, Detroit.

18. Tim Kiska, "Jerry Blocker Was TV Pioneer," *Detroit News*, November 5, 1997, E1.

19. Ibid.

20. Clark, interview.

21. Kiska, "Jerry Blocker Was TV Pioneer," E1.

22. Author's interview with William Serrin, April 13, 2003.

23. De Lisle, interview.

24. Kalush, interview.

25. Ibid.

26. *Report of the National Advisory Commission on Civil Disorders*, 88.

27. Author's interview with Ira Rosenberg, April 13, 2003.

28. *News Media Coverage of the 1967 Urban Riots*, Final Report, prepared by Dr. Sol Chaneles, project director, February 1, 1968, 9, series 41, box 9, LBJ.

29. "When Dawn Came, a Restless Truce Seemed to Envelop the Area," *Detroit News*, August 11, 1967, *A Time of Tragedy* special section, 11.

30. Kalush, interview.

31. Author's interview with Jim Herrington, April 13, 2003.

32. Detroit broadcast transcripts, Kerner Commission, LBJ.

33. Kalush, interview.

34. Rosenberg, interview.

35. Kalush, interview.

36. WXYZ-TV tape (in author's possession).

37. Kalush, interview.

38. Tim Kiska, "The Million-Dollar Man," *Detroit News*, May 15, 1991, H1.

39. Kalush, interview.

40. "The Aftermath," series 41, box 6, LBJ.

41. Sidney Fine, *Violence in the Model City: The Cavanagh Administration, Race Relations, and the Detroit Riot of 1967* (Ann Arbor: University of Michigan Press, 1989), 358.

42. *Detroit Free Press*, July 25, 1967, 8B.

43. Frank Judge, "TV, Radio Praised for Riot Coverage," *Detroit News*, July 25, 1967, 18A.

44. Author's interview with Dwayne X. Riley, May 12, 2003.

45. Ibid.

46. John F. Day, introduction to *CBS News: Television News Reporting* (New York: McGraw-Hill, 1958), 1.

47. Kalush, interview.

48. Riley, interview.

49. "Detroit Papers Publish after 9-Month Shutdown," *New York Times*, August 10, 1968,

50. *New York Times*, November 26, 1964, 68.

51. *New York Times*, March 3, 1968, 30.

52. Herrington, interview.

53. Jack R. Hendrickson, "Public Television Management, Financing and Programming at

Station WTVS-TV/Channel 56, Detroit 1966–1980," master's thesis, Wayne State University, 1986, 59.

54. "Senator Estes Kefauver, Tennessee Democrat, Is Dead at 60 After Heart Attack," *New York Times*, August 11, 1963, 86.

55. Pete Waldmeir, "Lou Gordon—A Unique Personality," *Detroit News*, May 25, 1977, C8.

56. "Lou Gordon: Man of Conscience, Man of Truth," available on DVD from www.detroitkidshow.com.

57. Ibid.

58. Lou Gordon, interview with George Romney, WKBD-TV (transcript in author's possession).

59. Author's interview with Jeanne Findlater, July 21, 2003.

CHAPTER 5

1. Leonard Goldenson, *Beating the Odds* (New York: Charles Scribner's Sons, 1991), 375.

2. ABC Annual Report, 1975, 10, available at ProQuest Historical Annual Reports, http://www.proquest.com/products_pq/descriptions/pq_hist_annual_repts.shtml.

3. Goldenson, *Beating the Odds*, 377.

4. Ron Powers, *The Newscasters* (New York: St. Martin's, 1977), 147.

5. Ibid., 151.

6. Fred Ferretti, "'Eyewitness News' Causing Change at Other Stations," *New York Times*, December 10, 1970.

7. John J. O'Connor, "TV: The Enduring Success of 'Eyewitness News,'" *New York Times*, February 9, 1972, 79.

8. John Kelly and Marilyn Turner, *Good Morning Detroit: The*

Kelly & Co. Story (Chicago: Contemporary, 1986), 62.

9. Ibid., 64.

10. McHugh and Hoffman, Inc., "Essential Findings and Recommendations for WJBK-TV," September 8, 1969, 23, 24, McHugh and Hoffman files, Bentley Historical Library, University of Michigan, Ann Arbor.

11. O'Connor, "TV: The Enduring Success of 'Eyewitness News,'" 79.

12. Barbara Campbell, "Melba? She's the Toast of the Town," *New York Times*, February 18, 1973.

13. *Detroit News*, March 10, 2001, E1.

14. Ibid.

15. Ibid.

16. Author's interview with Phil Nye, May 12, 2003.

17. Av Westin, *Newswatch: How TV Decides the News* (New York: Simon & Schuster, 1982), 222.

18. Powers, *The Newscasters*, 183.

19. Westin, *Newswatch*, 22.

20. John J. O'Connor, "TV: Willowbrook State School, 'the Big Town's Leper Colony,'" *New York Times*, February 2, 1972.

21. Kelly and Turner, *Good Morning Detroit*, 97.

22. Ibid., 94.

23. Nye, interview.

24. *Electronic Media*, May 27, 2002, 9.

25. Nye, interview.

26. John J. Connor, "TV: Battle behind News," *New York Times*, March 8, 1974.

27. American Broadcasting Companies Annual Report, 1977, 2, available at ProQuest Historical Annual Reports, http://www.proquest.com/products_pq/descriptions/pq_hist_annual_repts.shtml.

28. O'Connor, "TV: Battle behind News."

29. Judy Klemesrud, "Anchorwomen: Late Break in Local News," *New York Times*, January 22, 1980.

30. Campbell, "Melba?"

31. Powers, *The Newscasters*, 184

32. Les Brown, "Livelier and Longer TV News Spurts Hunt for Talent," *New York Times*, April 22, 1974.

33. John J. O'Connor, "TV: Stokes and Udell, the New News Team in Town," *New York Times*, May 24, 1972.

34. Author's interview with Dwayne X. Riley, May 12, 2003.

35. Author's interview with Betty Carrier, April 16, 2007.

36. Ibid.

37. Bettelou Peterson, "Soft Ratings Forced WWJ News Switch," *Detroit Free Press*, November 21, 1973, 5B.

CHAPTER 6

1. Jerry M. Flint, "Paper in Detroit Turns Fortress," *New York Times*, November 17, 1968.

2. Ibid.

3. Ibid.

4. William W. Lutz, *The News of Detroit* (Boston: Little, Brown, 1973), 91.

5. Steven V. Roberts, "At Half Time in Football, a Big and Costly Show," *New York Times*, January 2, 1972.

6. Author's interview with Louis Prato, June 30, 2003.

7. Don F. DeGroot, *Living on Air* (self-published book in author's possession), 426.

8. "Rape Try Thwarted by Sound of Brakes," Crime in Detroit, *Detroit News*, September 10, 1968, 3A.

9. Lutz, *The News of Detroit*, 146.

10. Social Research, Inc., "Television in the Greater Detroit Area, Late Winter 1968," Spring 1968, 74, McHugh and Hoffman files, Bentley Historical Library, University of Michigan, Ann Arbor.

11. DeGroot, *Living on Air*, 432.

12. Prato, interview.

13. Reuven Frank, *Out of Thin Air* (New York: Simon & Schuster, 1991), 296, 326.

14. DeGroot, *Living on Air*, 432.

15. WWJ-TV press release, October 15, 1975, Fred E. Dohrs biographical file, Archives of Labor and Urban Affairs, Walter P. Reuther Library, Detroit.

16. Ibid.

17. Ibid.

18. Ibid.

19. Prato, interview.

20. DeGroot, *Living on Air*, 448.

21. Author's telephone interview with James F. Clark, July 2, 2003.

22. McHugh and Hoffman, Inc., "The Detroit TV Market in the Fall of 1968," November 18, 1968, 44–45, McHugh and Hoffman files, Bentley Historical Library, University of Michigan, Ann Arbor.

23. Peter S. Hoffman, "Essential Finds and Recommendations For WJBK-TV," May 24, 1974, 8, McHugh and Hoffman files, Bentley Historical Library, University of Michigan, Ann Arbor.

24. James Harper, "Ch. 4 Fires Ackerman for Comment on Olympics," *Detroit Free Press*, September 10, 1972, 1, 16A.

25. DeGroot, *Living on Air*, 449.

26. Ibid., 452.

27. Prato, interview.

28. Ibid.

29. Ibid

30. Ibid.

CHAPTER 7

1. Ernest Holsendolph, "Court Bars Papers from Owning Radio or TV in Same City," *New York Times*, March 2, 1977.

2. Deirdre Carmody, "A Way Out Is Seen for Press-TV Cross-Ownership," *New York Times*, December 13, 1977.

3. Warren Weaver Jr., "Court Upholds Ban on Press Acquiring TV or Radio Outlets," *New York Times*, June 13, 1978.

4. David Eden, "New Owner Takes over WWJ-TV with Sign-on," *Detroit News*, June 26, 1978, 1A.

5. Harrison S. Wyman, "Appreciation: The Influence of Jim Snyder," April 21, 2001, Washington, DC/Baltimore TV News, http://www.geocities.com/dcbaltotvnews/wyman/index.htm (accessed March 20, 2003).

6. Author's interview with Terrence Oprea, July 1, 2003.

7. Author's interview with Bob Allison, July 31, 2000.

8. Marc Gunther, *The House That Roone Built: The Inside Story of ABC News* (Boston: Little, Brown, 1994), 70.

9. Oprea, interview.

10. Katherine Graham, *Personal History* (New York: Alfred A. Knopf, 1997), 583.

11. Mike Duffy, " 'Free 4 All' Is Fizzy—and Fun," *Detroit Free Press*, June 19, 1981, 10D.

12. Robert Pisor, *The End of the Line: The Siege of Khe Sanh* (New York: W. W. Norton, 1982).

13. Author's telephone interview with Dick Haefner, May 21, 2008.

14. Oprea, interview.

15. Ibid.

16. Ellen Creager, "Captive of Cocaine: Ben Frazier," *Detroit Free Press*, April 26, 1988, 1B.

17. Ben Brown, "The Bottom Line: Frazier Brouhaha Boils Down to One Thing: Money," *Detroit News*, October 16, 1981, D9.

18. McHugh and Hoffman, Inc., "Essential Findings and Recommendations For WJBK-TV," June 8, 1973, 2, 8, 28, McHugh and Hoffman files, Bentley Historical Library, University of Michigan, Ann Arbor.

19. Ibid, 28.

20. "TV News Reporter Baxter Ward Enters Race for Mayor of L.A.," *Los Angeles Times*, January 5, 1969.

21. Dan Knapp, "Front-runners in L.A.'s TV News Sweepstakes," *Los Angeles Times*, December 11, 1969.

22. "And Now Here's Jerry, Bob, Bill, Tom, George and Baxter," *Los Angeles Times*, May 3, 1970.

23. "Benti Will Head KABC Newscast," *Los Angeles Times*, March 9, 1971.

24. McHugh and Hoffman, Inc., "Essential Findings and Recommendations for WJBK-TV," November 18, 1968, 3, McHugh and Hoffman files, Bentley Historical Library, University of Michigan, Ann Arbor.

25. Josef Steven Olsavsky, "Influences of News Programming Techniques and News Market Conditions in Detroit on the Restructuring of WJBK-TV News, 1981–1983" (MA thesis, Michigan State University, 1984), 59.

26. John Kelly and Marilyn Turner, *Good Morning Detroit: The Kelly & Co. Story* (Chicago: Contemporary, 1986), 66.

27. Author's interview with Henry Baskin, April 18, 2007.

28. Bettelou Peterson, "Jac LeGoff Going to Channel 7," *Detroit Free Press*, July 10, 1974, 1A.

29. Philip L. McHugh, "Viewer Attitudes toward Local News Teams," Spring 1975, 6, 11, McHugh and Hoffman files, Bentley Historical Library, University of Michigan, Ann Arbor.

30. Ibid, 17.

31. Olsavsky, "Influences of News Programming Techniques," 4.

32. Author's interview with Murray Feldman, April 15, 2007.

33. Ibid.

34. Author's interview with Marla Drutz, May 28, 2003 (notes in author's possession).

35. Author's telephone interview with Joe Glover, May 28, July 14, 2003.

36. Peter S. Hoffman, "Essential Findings and Recommendations—Detroit Market Study," Winter 1979, box 103809, McHugh and Hoffman files, Bentley Historical Library, University of Michigan, Ann Arbor.

37. Ibid., 7, 16.

38. Ibid., 24, 6.

39. Olsavsky, "Influences of News Programming Techniques," 74.

40. Pete Waldmeir, "TV 2 Deserves Lumps for Way It Fired Sonny Eliot," *Detroit News*, July 23, 1982, B1.

41. Glover, interview, July 14, 2003.

42. Lee Thornton, e-mail to author, April 14, 2007.

43. Ibid.

44. Ben Brown, "She Eagerly Puts Detroit Behind Her," *Detroit News*, July 11, 1982, 2E.

45. Thornton, e-mail.

EPILOGUE

1. Capital Cities/ABC, Incorporated Annual Report—1985,28; available at available at ProQuest Historical Annual Reports, http://www.proquest.com/products_pq/descriptions/pq_hist_annual_repts.shtml.

2. Bill Abrams, "Capital Cities, ABC to Sell 2 TV Outlets to Scripps Howard Unit for $246 million," *Wall Street Journal*, July 29, 1985.

3. Sonia L. Nazario and Steve Swartz, "Storer Board Accepts $2.51 Billion Bid from Kohlberg, Kravis, Spurns Comcast," *Wall Street Journal*, July 31, 1985.

4. "FCC Affirms Buyout of Storer by Division of Kohlberg Kravis," *Wall Street Journal*, November 26, 1985.

5. Peter W. Barnes, "Building a TV Station Empire on Debt," *Wall Street Journal*, April 13, 1987.

6. Laura Landro, "Lorimar Is Said Planning to Buy 7 TV Stations," *Wall Street Journal*, May 21, 1986; Peter W. Barnes and Michael Cieply, "Lorimar Drops Plan to Buy TV Stations For $1.41 Billion, with Kohlberg Assent," *Wall Street Journal*, November 13, 1986.

7. Bill Carter, "Networks Jolting: Big Realignment Shifts Strong Affiliates into Murdoch's System," *New York Times*, May 24, 1994.

8. Geraldine Fabrikant, "Murdoch Bets Heavily on a Global Vision," *New York Times*, July 29, 1996.

9. Bill Carter, "CBS Buys 2 UHF Stations to Serve Atlanta and Detroit," *New York Times*, September 24, 1994.

10. Dale Parry, "CBS Gets OK at Channel 62," *Detroit Free Press*, July 25, 1995, 4E.

11. Daniel J. Boorstin, *The Image: A Guide to Pseudo-Events in America* (New York: Atheneum, 1987), 8.

12. Norman Sinclair, "Bonds Brawls in Bar," *Detroit News*, January 31, 1990, A1.

13. Vivian S. Toy, "Bonds Settle Traffic Bills," *Detroit News*, December 29, 1987, B1.

14. Denise Crittendon, "A New Round in Bonds-Young Feud: Let's Fight," *Detroit News*, July 16, 1989, A1.

15. N. Scott Vance and Tim Kiska, "Bill Bonds in Calif. Alcohol Treatment Center," *Detroit News*, August 12, 1989, A1; Pat McCaughan and Liz Twardon, " 'It Is Great to Be Back, It Is Even Greater to Be Sober,' " *Detroit News*, August 29, 1989, A1.

16. *Detroit News Index* (Ann Arbor, MI: University Microfilms International, 1989), 158; search of *www.freepress.com*, January 1, 1994–December 31, 1994.

17. Tim Kiska and Elizabeth Atkins, "Bill Bonds Jailed for Drunken Driving," *Detroit News*, August 8, 1994, A1; Tim Kiska, "Ratings King Has Had a Long Fall from Grace," *Detroit News*, August 9 1994, A1; Mike Martindale, "Bonds May Be Hospitalized for Alcoholism Treatment," *Detroit News*, August 10, 1994.

18. Tim Kiska, "Channel 2 Pulls Anchorman After Use of Cars Questioned," *Detroit News*, November 28, 1995, A1.

19. Tim Kiska, "Channel 2's Pierce Drove 99 Free Cars in 1994–95," *Detroit News*, November 29, 1995, A1; "Bonds Gets Fired: Flashy Anchor Says He'll Be Back on TV," *Detroit Free Press*, January 12, 1995, 1; Tim Kiska, "Fired Anchor Bonds Vows to Return to TV—'Absolutely,' " *Detroit News*, January 12, 1995, A1.

20. Tim Kiska, "Hatch Stalks out of Interview After Bonds Slams Thomas Panel," *Detroit News*, October 17, 1991, A1.

21. Tim Kiska, "Local TV News Shows Hooked on Violence," *Detroit News*, February 16, 1997, 1A.

22. Sally Bedell Smith, *In All His Glory* (New York: Simon & Schuster, 1990), 166.

23. Bill Leonard, *In the Storm of the Eye: A Lifetime at CBS* (New York: G. P. Putnam's Sons, 1987), 33.

24. Ibid.

25. Edward Bliss Jr., ed., *In Search of Light: The Broadcasts of Edward R. Murrow* (New York: Alfred A. Knopf, 1967), 360.

Note: Italicized page numbers indicate tables, figures or photographs.

public service programming, 54
public television station, 76

racism, 64–65, 68–69, 93–94
radio: advertising on, 5; as amusement,
    1–2; journalism, xv, 1, 8–12; legacy
    of, 21, 37; network, as sideshow,
    43; newscasters, 2–5, 7; newspaper
    companies and, 2, 4; orchestras, 2,
    4, *105–6*; production of AM sets,
    18; profitability of, 41–42; revenue
    and income, Detroit stations, 62,
    155, *166*; revenue and income,
    nationwide, *156*; rock music
    scandal, 36. *See also* radio stations
Radio Corporation of America (RCA),
    13, 16
radio stations: ABC-owned, xiv, 82;
    cross-ownership of, 6, 19, 21, 31, 36;
    raid on, for news talent, 60. *See also*
    individual radio stations
Radio-Television News Directors
    Association, xiii
Rather, Dan, 145
ratings: and advertising revenue, 134;
    among black households, 11 p.m.,
    95; Monday–Friday, 11 p.m., 75,
    90–91; pressure on local television
    for, 145–46; and shares, 11 p.m.,
    101, 130. *See also individual television
    stations*
Rayburn, Sam, 16
RCA (Radio Corporation of America),
    13, 16
Reid, Whitelaw, 44
religious programming, 38
reporters: African American, 84–85;
    backgrounds of earliest, 31–35; beat
    system for, 29–30; for *Detroit News*,
    during newspaper strike, 93; in early
    TV days, 25; on-air, 32, 128; and
    television news program, 76
research: television and, xiii, xvii, 11,
    49–55, 94; for WJBK-TV by Peter
    Hoffman, 98
Reuther, Walter P., 58
Richards, George A., 11

Riley, Dwayne X., 33–34, 73–74
rip and read, 26, 28
Ripley, Anthony, 68
Rivera, Geraldo, 85–86, 88
Robinson, Edward J., 68, 182 n.15
Robinson, Max, 126–27
rock music radio scandal, 36–37
Rocky Mountain Media Watch,
    xvi, 144
Rojas, Gloria, 85
Romney, George, 48, 58, 65, 76,
    78–79, *118*
Rosenberg, Ira, 70
Ruth, Babe, *103*
Ryan, Harold J., 21

Salant, Richard S., 46, 48–49, 86
Sales, Soupy, 27, 39
Salisbury, Harrison, 48
Sarnoff, David, 13
Savitch, Jessica, 127
Scamardella, Rose Ann, 85–86, 88
Schecter, Abel A., 8
Schiavone, James, 67
SCI Television, Inc., 140–41
Scripps, James E., 18–19
Scripps, William E., 6, 17–18, *113*,
    116, *122*
Scripps, William J., *116*, *122–23*
Scripps family, 18–19
Scripps Howard Broadcasting
    Company, 140
See It Now (TV news show), 47
Selection Research Institute, 137
Serrin, William, 69
Sessa, Mike, 128
Sevareid, Eric, 10, 42, 48
Shirer, William L., 9–10
Shorr, Mickey, 36
Shurmur, E. L. "Hank," 34–35
Siegal, Sid, 25
Simmons, Larry, 128
Sinnott, Arthur, 4
Sirica, John J., 22
Smilovitz, Bernie, 141
Smith, Carl E., 70
Smith, Howard K., 9–10, 57–58

WTVS-TV, 181 n.5

WWDT-TV, 14–15, 19

WWJ-AM: Carl Cederberg and, 32; control room of, *105*; newscast viewers, *171*; orchestra of, *106*; orders from ENA on antiwar demonstration, 93; programming of, 18–19; recording studio of, *104*; studios of, *110*; World Series broadcast, *111*

WWJ-radio, 1–2, 4, 10, 19

WWJ-TV: Al Ackerman and, 98–100; acquisition of, by *Washington Post*, 126; appearance of weaknesses in, 54; Bob Bennett and, 84; Jerry Blocker and, 68–69; conservative point of view, 92, 98; debut of, 17, 38; *Detroit News* and, 92–93; and Detroit riot, 67, 73–75; early days of, 22–23, 26; election desk, *118*; Jac Le Goff at anchor desk of, *120*; Kirk Knight and, 31; live broadcasts, 28–29, 48, *111*; market power of, 52; Phil McHugh on problems of, 94; newscasts, local, 31–35, 55–56, *153*, *163–64*; news operation of, 29–30, 100–101; news ratings, xvi, 90–91, 95, 102, *160*, *168*; newsroom morale at, 101; and NLU Productions, 34; profitability of, 41; sale of, 125; and television news as show business, 89–90; test pattern of, *110*. *See also* WDIV-TV

WXYZ-AM, 21, 36

WXYZ-TV: anchor selection, 58–59; Doris Biscoe and, 85; Bill Bonds and, 131; coverage of Detroit riot, 70–73; debut of, 17, 22, 38; emulation of WABC-TV, 88; gains of, in 1970s, 131; goodwill, loss of, 75; Don Haney and, 68; marketing campaign to promote news team, 133; Mr. Weather on, 35; newscasts, 24, 28, 31–35, 55–57, 61–62; newscasts, time slot and duration, 30, 56, *154*, *165*; news image, 136; news operation, 27; news ratings, 95, *160*, *168*, *172*; on-air news personalities of, 132; ownership changes, 20, 140; profitability of, xviii, 28; staff raids by, xii, 60; viewers, *171*

Wyman, Harrison S., 126

W*Y*X*I*E Wonderland (Osgood), 39

Young, Coleman A., 73

Young, Dale, 36

Young, Murray, 26

Your Show of Shows, 38

ZeVan, Barry, 136

Zieve, Mort, 23

Zimmerman, Dave, 14–15, *121*